Should Babies be Baptized?

Should Babies be Baptized?

T. E. Watson

Grace Publications

Original Edition   *Baptism not for infants*
       © T.E. Watson   1962
This Edition 1995

© Grace Publications Trust 1995
139 Grosvenor Ave
London N5 2NH
England

ISBN 0 9464 62 36 4

Joint Managing Editors
J.P. Arthur M.A.
H.J.Appleby

Distributed by:
EVANGELICAL PRESS
12 Wooler Street
Darlington
Co Durham DL1 1RQ
England

Cover design: L.L.Evans

Printed in Great Britain by The Bath Press, Avon

Contents

Foreword

'Then came his disciples, and said unto him, Knowest thou that the Pharisees were offended, after they heard this saying? But he answered and said, Every plant, which my heavenly Father hath not planted, shall be rooted up' (Matt. 15:12,13).

Our Lord's conduct here shows that we are not from the fear of giving offence ... to refrain from speaking the truth, especially with regard to doctrine and usages, unsanctioned by divine authority, which men endeavour to impose as articles of faith and religious observances, and by which they cast into the shade doctrines plainly revealed, and substantially make void ordinances clearly appointed by the Lord.

It is no uncommon thing, when the truth on these subjects is spoken, however calmly, for persons ... to be dissatisfied and offended. And some very well-intended persons, like the disciples, are disposed to say, It is a pity — would it not have been better to avoid such subjects?

But is the truth to be concealed? This would be, on the part of him who knows it, unkindness to his mistaken brethren, injustice to truth, treason against the God of truth. To all men, especially to well-meaning though mistaken brethren in Christ, we ought to avoid giving unnecessary offence. We ought to be ready to sacrifice personal comfort to a great extent, rather than incur this evil. 'If meat make my brother to fall, I will eat no more meat while the world standeth'.

But we must not sacrifice a jot or tittle of Christ's truth to gain this or any other end, however apparently desirable. The 'teaching for doctrines the commandments of men' — the 'making void God's commandment of men's traditions' we must clearly expose and strongly condemn, undiverted from our course by the fear of shocking the prejudices even of those genuine Christians who have been entangled in the snares of any of those systems where man holds the place of God, however much we may love their persons, and value what is genuine in their Christian faith and character. This is kindness to them, as well as justice to truth.

With regard to everything in the shape of religious doctrine, which we cannot find in the Bible — with regard to everything in the shape of religious institutions, unsanctioned by divine authority — we must 'lift up our voices like a trumpet', and proclaim, whosoever may be offended, 'Every plant which our heavenly Father hath not planted,' should — must — 'shall, be rooted up'.

John Brown

(Discourses and Sayings of our Lord, Vol. 1, p. 499F.)

Preface

Some may think that this is no time to publish a book on the baptism of babies. The decadent state of the churches, the desperate situation in the world, the vast work of evangelism facing a handful of Evangelicals, demand that Christians devote all their energy to the things that matter most. To start people arguing about whether babies are to be baptized is to set Christians fiddling while Christendom burns!

That the baptism of babies is not a matter of primary importance I readily agree. True, there are some who think of believers' baptism more highly than they ought to think, and not only too highly but too frequently, riding their hobbyhorse ad nauseam. I have every sympathy with those who protest, 'First things first!' Nonetheless, is the putting of first things first any excuse for not putting second things second? When our Lord rebuked the Pharisees for neglecting the weightier matters of the law, he never excused them from paying attention to the lighter matters. On the contrary, he said, 'These ought ye to have done, and not leave the other undone' (Matthew 23:23).

That this book will start Christians arguing about the baptizing of babies I deny. The fact is that they already argue about it, and have been doing so for centuries. Should this book provoke more controversy, I shall not mind, provided it is conducted in a spirit of meekness and love. Controversy marks the presence of deep convictions and, generally, thinking minds. If controversy sets men searching the Scriptures, it is by no means a bad thing.

I do not expect to convince everyone who considers the arguments contained in these pages, but I unashamedly declare that this is my aim. If I did not seek to convince others of what I believe, it would indicate that I was not fully persuaded myself. If I am convinced that the baptism of babies is a gross perversion of one of the ordinances of Christ, am I not entitled, rather, is it not my duty, to oppose it with the same energy displayed by our illustrious Reformers when resisting the Romanist's perversion of the other ordinance? Is the perversion of Christian baptism less sacrilegious than the perversion of the Lord's Supper? Both are ordinances of Christ, and both ought to be observed in their original purity.

Of the multitudes who believe in baptizing babies very few have ever seriously considered the reasons for their belief. The majority receive it by tradition from their fathers with very little thought. My heart's desire is that such will start searching the Scriptures diligently until they know for themselves whether baptizing babies is from heaven or of men. Then there are others who have investigated the subject without coming to any sure conclusion. And it may be there are some who have come to a sure conclusion without having examined all the evidence. Such as these obviously need to reconsider their position. Should any Christian, however, after diligent study and due thought, remain fully persuaded that the baptism of babies is authorized by Scripture, I agree to disagree with him without being disagreeable. I will continue to love him as a brother for whom Christ died.

It will not be out of place, I trust, to relate how I came to my present convictions and to write this book. Christened and confirmed in the Church of England, educated at a College with a High Church tradition, I was bent for the Anglican ministry. Then I was converted. Being now regenerate, I not unnaturally began to question the statements in the Prayer Book declaring the regeneration of those baptized. These proved to be knots which even good Bishop Ryle failed to untie — at least to my satisfaction — and eventually for conscience' sake I had to leave what is commonly reckoned to be 'the best boat to fish from.'

Reacting against the teaching of the Prayer Book, I was very disposed to reject the baptism of babies altogether. Then I was introduced to the Puritans whose writings I devoured with great delight. At last I found literature which really satisfied my soul.

Discovering the Puritans to be right on so many points, I thought they must have very good reasons for baptizing babies. Who am I, I thought, to disagree with theological giants like John Owen and Thomas Goodwin?

The covenant theology of the Puritans was hard to understand, but it sounded impressive and seemed convincing, and I thought I should understand it in due course. I did ... but not in the way expected. I well remember a Puritan Studies Conference at Westminster Chapel when an excellent paper was read by Dr. J.I. Packer on *The Baptismal Controversy among the Puritans.* I was almost persuaded — until the ensuing discussion threw me into a greater confusion than ever. I left the Conference in a whirl. How complicated it all seemed. Would I ever come to a definite conclusion? There was so much to study and consider that I began to despair and nearly gave up. But I had to go on because until I had solved this problem I could not determine the sphere of my future ministry.

The next stage in my pilgrimage was the realisation that if I had any doubt as to the scripturalness of baptizing babies, I could never practise the same with a good conscience. 'Whatsoever is not of faith is sin' (Romans 14:23). He that doubts, yet still baptizes babies, is condemned, because he does not do it of faith. It was helpful to realize that as long as I was unpersuaded one way or the other, I could not baptize babies without sinning against my conscience and incurring condemnation.

In the providence of God I had two years to serve in the Army which afforded me ample opportunity for study. Soon I became more conversant with Puritan terminology and more able to follow their arguments and to detect their fallacies. Their whole case finally collapsed when I read a borrowed copy of Alexander Carson's *Baptism, its Mode and Subjects.* I was not very interested in the mode of baptism — that is another question entirely — but Carson's examination of the covenant with Abraham brought the longed-for light. The fog had gone.

Eager to impart my discovery to others, I wrote a booklet entitled *Twenty Questions Concerning Infant Baptism* which I had duplicated. When the first edition was exhausted, certain friends urged me to enlarge it and have it printed. But I declined on the grounds that I had more important work to attend to. However, the continued re-issue of commentaries and works of theology favouring the baptism of babies caused me to realize the urgent need for someone to write a thorough refutation of the theory and practice. To my knowledge no such refutation had been written in this generation, so I gave myself to further study and research, and the booklet grew into the book now in the reader's hands.

A word of explanation is needed concerning the great number of quotations which the reader will meet with in the following pages. It has been my policy to support my various points with quotations from writers believing in the baptism of babies, (hereafter called Paedobaptists). In fact it will be found that all the quotations adduced are taken from Paedobaptist writings. The reason for doing this is obvious, 'This testimony of theirs, to me, is worth a thousand others; seeing it comes from such as, in my opinion, are evidently interested to speak quite otherwise.' (Daille.) The practice of quoting one's opponents is not without apostolic precedent. When Paul disputed with the Athenians he thought it fair and fitting to say, 'As certain also of your own poets have said' (Acts 17:28).

In adopting this policy of reinforcing my points with quotes from Paedopbaptist authors, there is the obvious danger of misquotation which, let me hasten to say, I have conscientiously sought to avoid. My purpose in using certain quotations is to establish the point under consideration, not the conclusion which I draw from the point. It need hardly be said that not infrequently the author quoted does not endorse the conclusion I draw from his quotation; in fact, he may contradict it. In these cases the reader has to decide if my conclusion is a good and necessary one.

Instead of relegating the quotations to the foot of the page where they would very likely be overlooked, I have included them in the actual text, at the same time keeping my own remarks to a minimum. As a result the book takes on a certain patchwork appearance. However, I trust that there will be no lack of coherence.

Some of the quotations are so surprising that many will wonder how anyone could concede so much and remain a Paedobaptist. The explanation is that 'Reformed theologians did not all agree in the past, and are not even now all unanimous, in their representation of the ground of infant baptism.' (L. Berkhof, *Systematic Theology*, p. 639) Or, in the words of B.B. Warfield, 'We do not all argue alike.' (*Studies in Theology*, p.406.) Those who build on one foundation are generally quite willing to yield the ground that others build on. As an old writer remarked concerning the Jewish Rabbis, 'When men dispute against the truth, what one of them builds up is presently pulled down by another.' Other of the quotations are taken from passages where the author is arguing *against* the indiscriminate baptism of adults or *for* the necessity of sponsors or godparents.

While I have not quoted any Baptist (more strictly Anti-paedobaptist) writers, I have nevertheless read their works and entered into their labours. Gratitude compels me to record my inestimable debt to Abraham Booth's 'Paedobaptism Examined on the Principles, Concessions, and Reasonings of the Most Learned Paedobaptists'- an apt description of the method of this present work, except that unlike Booth I have confined myself to the *subject* of baptism. Then there is R.Ingham's invaluable *Christian Baptism: Its Subjects* which, as a handbook on baptism, stands unrivalled for its wealth of information and orderliness of presentation. Both books are to be found in the Evangelical Library, 78a Chiltern Street, London, W1M 2BH.

Among the many friends who have made helpful suggestions and offered valuable assistance, I would particularly mention Mr. Paul Helm and the Rev. R.J.Graham. Their kind labours are appreciated.

Because of the importance of reading the following pages in the right frame of mind, I will conclude this preface with an extract from the famous speech of the Puritan Paedobaptist, John Robinson, which he addressed to the Pilgrim Fathers in 1620 just prior to their setting sail for the New World:

> I charge you before God and before his blessed angels, that you follow me no further than you have seen me follow the Lord Jesus Christ. If God reveal anything to you by any other instrument of his, be as ready to receive it as ever you were to receive any truth by my ministry; for I am verily persuaded, I am very confident, the Lord hath more truth yet to break forth out of his holy Word. For my part, I cannot sufficiently bewail the condition of the reformed churches, who are come to a period* in religion; and will go at present, no further than the instruments of their first reformation. The Lutherans cannot be drawn to go beyond what Luther saw: whatever

part of his will our good God has imparted and revealed unto Calvin, they will rather die than embrace it. And the Calvinists, you see, stick fast where they were left by that great man of God; who yet saw not all things. This is a misery much to be lamented; for though they were burning and shining lights in their times, yet they penetrated not into the whole counsel of God: but were they now living, they would be as willing to embrace further light, as that which they first received' (J.Fletcher's *History of Independency*, vol. 3, p. 69.)

* *i.e. full stop.*

T. E. Watson.

Addendum 1969

H.M. Carson, whose commentary is quoted on page ...., is no longer a paedobaptist. How he came to change his mind is described in a chapter on baptism in *Farewell to Anglicanism* (published by Henry E. Walter Ltd).

Index of Paedobaptist Works Quoted

Alexander, J.A., *Commentary on the Acts of the Apostles* (Zondervan).

Alford, H., *Greek New Testament.*

Bannerman, J., *The Church of Christ* (Banner of Truth Trust).

Barnes, A., *Commentary on the New Testament* (Baker Book House).

Bartlett, J.V., *The Apostolic Age.*

Baxter, Richard, *Certain Disputations of Right to Sacrament, Plain Scripture Proof of Infants Church Membership and Baptism, Practical Works.*

Berkhof, L., *Systematic Theology* (Eerdmans & Banner of Truth Trust).

Bickersteth, E., *On Baptism.*

Bingham, J., *Antiquities of the Christian Church.*

Boston, Thomas, *Works.*

Bromiley, G.W., *The Baptism of Infants* (Church Book Room Press).

Brown, D., *Commentary on the Bible* by Jamieson, Fausset and Brown, 6 vols., (Eerdmans).

Brown, John (of Edinburgh) *Discourses and Sayings of our Lord.*

Burkitt, W., *Commentary on the New Testament.*

Burnet, Bishop, Gibson's *Preservative from Popery* (18 vol. edn.).

Calvin, J., *Harmony of the Gospels* (Eerdmans), Commentary on Acts (Eerdmans).

Carson, H.M., *Commentary on Colossians and Philemon* Tyndale Press).

Clagett, W., Gibson's *Preservative from Popery.*

Clarke, Adam, *Commentary on the Bible* (Abingdon).

Cunningham, W., Article in the *British and Foreign Evangelical Quarterly* (1860), *Historical Theology* (Banner of Truth Trust), *The Reformers and the Theology of the Reformation.*

Doddridge, Philip, *Paraphrase of the New Testament, Miscellaneous Works.*

Eadie, J., *Biblical Cylopaedia.*

Edersheim, A., *Life and Times of Jesus the Messiah* (Longmans).

Edwards, Jonathan, *Enquiry into Qualifications for Full Communion.*

Edwards, Peter, *Candid reasons for Renouncing the Principles of Antipaedobaptism.*

Erskine, John, *Theological Dissertations.*

Fairbairn, P., *Imperial Bible Dictionary* (Zondervan), *Typology of Scripture* (Oliphants).

Fletcher. J., *History of Independency.*

Foakes-Jackson, F.J., *History of the Christian Church* (Allenson).

Griffith-Thomas, W.H., *The Catholic Faith* (Church Book Room Press).

Guthrie, Thomas, *The Gospel in Ezekiel.*

Hagenbach, K.R., *History of Doctrines* (T. & T. Clark).

Hammond, H., *Six Queries of Present Use in the Church of England, Works.*

Hendriksen, W., *The Gospel of John* (Baker Book House & Banner of Truth).

Henry, Matthew, *Commentry on the Bible* (Marshall, Morgan & Scott), *Treatise on Baptism.*

Hodge, A.A., *Confession of Faith* (Banner of Truth Trust), *Outlines of Theology* (Eerdmans).

Hodge, Charles, *Commentary on Romans* (Eerdmans). *Systematic Theology* [Eerdmans & Jas. Clarke], *The Way of Life* (Banner of Truth Trust).

James, J.A., *Principles of Dissent and Duties of Dissenters.*

Lange, J., *Commentary on Matthew* (T. & T. Clarke).

Lange, L., *History of Protestantism.*

Leighton, R., *Select Works.*

Lightfoot, J.B., *Apostolic Fathers.*

Lindsay, T.M., *Article in Encyclopaedia Britannica* (9th edition).

Marcel, P., *The Biblical Doctrine of Infant Baptism* (Jas. Clarke).

McCrie, Thomas, *Lectures on Christian Baptism.*

McGiffert, H.C., *History of Christianity in the Apostolic Age* (T.& T. Clarke).

Murray, John, *Christian Baptism* (Baker Book House), *Commen tary on Romans* (Eerdmans & Marshall, Morgan & Scott).

Neander, A., *Church History* (T. & T. Clark).

Olshausen, J., *Commentary on Acts* (T. & T. Clark). *Commentary on Corinthians.*

Owen, John, *Enquiry into the Original Nature of Churches, The Person of Christ, Works* (Goold).

Plummer, A., *Article on baptism in Hastings Biblical Dictionary.*

Poole, M., *Annotations on the Bible.*

Ryle, J. C., *Knots Untied, Expository Thoughts on the Gospels* (Jas. Clarke).

Schaff, P., *History of the Apostolic Church.*

Scott, T., *Commentary on the Bible.*

Sherlock, W., Gibsons's *Preservative from Popery.*

Simeon, C., *Expository Outlines on the Bible* (Zondervan & Oliphants).

Smeaton, G., *The Doctrine of the Holy Spirit* (Banner of Truth Trust.

Stier, R., *The Words of Jesus* (T. & T. Clark).

Taylor, J., *Liberty of Prophesying.*

Turrentine, F., *Institutes of Theology.*

Vos, J. G., *Blue Banner Faith and Life.*

Wall, W., *History of Infant Baptism.*

Wardlaw, R., *The Scripture Argument, Dissertation on Baptism.*

Warfield, B. B., *Studies in Theology (1932).*

Watson, Thomas, *The Ten Commandments* (Banner of Truth Trust).

Westminster Assembly of Divines, *Annotations on Holy Scripture.*

Wilson, R., *Infant Baptism.*

Woods, L., *Lectures on Infant Baptism.*

Chapter 1
Did the Jews baptize babies?

It is frequently affirmed that when John the Baptist began his ministry the Jews were in the habit of baptizing the children of proselytes to the Jewish faith. For example, J.C. Ryle, writing in the latter part of the 19th century, states:

> 'I might show, from the writings of old Dr. Lightfoot, that the baptism of little children was a practice with which the Jews were perfectly familiar. When proselytes were received into the Jewish Church by baptism, before our Lord Jesus Christ came, their infants were received, and baptized with them, as a matter of course.' *(Knots Untied,* p. 100.)

This being the case, is it not reasonable to assume that John the Baptist and the apostles of Christ, who were all Jews, did likewise? Reasonable as this assumption may be, it is after all still an assumption, and an assumption is not proof. This Louis Berkhof admits:

> 'Even if this did happen, it would prove nothing so far as Christian baptism is concerned, but it would go to show that there was nothing strange in such a procedure.' *(Systematic Theology,* p. 635.)

Notice that it would *prove nothing.* Berkhof says '*if* this did happen' because it is by no means certain that the children of Jewish proselytes were baptized in pre-Christian times. Indeed, it has yet to be proved that the Jews of those times baptized even the *adult* proselytes.

In the 1889 edition of the Imperial Bible Dictionary (which has an introduction by J.C. Ryle), Patrick Fairbairn writes:

'Many of the more learned inquirers into biblical antiquities, including Buxtorf, Lightfoot, Selden, Schottgen, Wall, etc., have been of the opinion that the Jews were in the habit of admitting proselytes to the Jewish faith by an ordinance of baptism accompanying the rite of circumcision.

'Later and more discriminating investigations, however, have shown this view to be untenable. It may almost, indeed, be held fatal to it, that both Philo and Josephus, who on so many occasions refer to the religious opinions and practices of their countrymen, never once allude to any such initiatory baptismal rite; in Josephus the admission of strangers is expressly said to have been by circumcision and sacrifice (Ant. 13:9; 20:2); and there is the like silence respecting baptism in the apocryphal writings, in the Targums of Onkelos and of Jonathan. It were impossible to account for such general silence, if the practice had really existed at the time.

'There is no evidence of a Jewish proselyte baptism till about the fourth century of the Christian era, when it does appear as a custom already in use, but one not probably introduced till the end of the third century; and the statements of rabbinical writers respecting its pre-Christian, and even Mosaic institution, are mere assertions without proof.' (See the rest of his article on Baptism as to how he thinks the practice probably originated.)

Writing at the same time and to the same effect, T.M. Lindsay, the historian, says:

'The subject of the baptism of proselytes is one of the most hopelessly obscure in the whole round of Jewish antiquities, and can never be safely assumed in any argument; and the general results of investigation seem to   prove   that   the baptism of proselytes was not one of the Jewish ceremonies until long after the coming of Christ.' *(Encyclopaedia Britannica, 9th edition.)*

Investigations into this obscure subject have continued from the time of Fairbairn and Lindsay, and nowadays the majority of scholars, Baptists and Paedobaptists alike, agree that there is sufficient evidence to prove that Jewish proselytes baptism was known and practised during the last decades of the first century A.D. Whether or not the practice was known before the destruction of Jerusalem in A.D. 70 is still being debated. For the present we may say that we have no sure proof that the Jews baptized proselytes before the coming of Christ. This is admitted in the 'perhaps' of a recent advocate of baby baptism, Professor G.W.Bromiley:

'From the first century A.D., and perhaps earlier, the Jews themselves practised baptism for the initiation of proselytes, and they definitely included all existing children with their parents. Whether the Christians copied the Jews or the Jews the Christians need not concern us.' *(The Baptism of Infants,* p. 1.)

It should be noticed that in his last sentence Bromiley is unwilling to commit himself to the long-held argument of many Paedobaptists that the first Christians took over baptism of babies from the Jews. There is no historical evidence for this frequently made assertion.

Even if it could be proved beyond doubt that the Jews were in the habit of baptizing the children of proselytes before the coming of Christ, it would not necessarily follow, as we saw above, that the first Christians must have copied the Jews in this respect. The only way to establish that the Christians copied the Jews in the matter of baptizing babies is by examining the teaching and practice of the Church in the Apostolic age. Only if we find baby baptism in the Apostolic Church are we entitled to affirm that the first Christians copied the Jews.

Those who rest the case for baby baptism totally or partially on the existence of Jewish proselyte baptism, need to remember that, in the words of Edersheim:

'Unborn children of proselytes did not require to be baptized because they were born in holiness.' *(Life and Times of Jesus the Messiah,* vol. 2, p. 746.)

In other words, it was the custom of the Jews not to baptize any child born to parents subsequently to their proselytisation. If therefore the

Jewish practice favours the baptism of a Christian convert's children, it is diametrically opposed to the baptism of any babies born subsequent to his conversion. They are born in holiness, and therefore do not need it! Surely we expect the Christians to copy the Jews! Thus, the argument from proselyte baptism is a two-edged sword — it cuts both ways.

Dr. Hammond and other Puritan writers with him, considered Jewish proselyte baptism 'the true basis of infant baptism.' *(Six Queries,* p. 195.) Now to argue thus is a virtual admission that baby baptism can be established only by going outside of Scripture. It is clear that to appeal to tradition, to be Jewish or Christian, for 'the true basis of infant baptism', is to vitiate the Protestant principle of the sufficiency of Holy Scripture for all matters of faith and practice. As Pierre Marcel so rightly points out:

> 'As good Reformed Christians it is impossible for us to found infant baptism on extra-canonical texts, no matter how compelling their authority may be. In the Christian Reformed Church the baptism of infants must be established and justified biblically.' *(The Biblical Doctrine of Infant Baptism,* p. 21.)

Or, in the words of the old Reformed slogan, the Bible, and the Bible only, is the religion of Protestants. To that Bible we will now turn.

Chapter 2
Did John baptize babies?

The first baptisms we meet in the pages of Holy Scripture are those administered by John. He was a man 'sent from God' (John 1:6) to prepare the way of the Lord which he did by calling on men to repent (Matthew 3:2). Besides being called to preach repentance he was 'sent to baptize' (John 1:33), and multitudes 'were baptized of him in Jordan, confessing their sins' (Matthew 3:6).

Writing of baptism in its first institution, John Owen states:

'God calls a man in a marvellous and miraculous manner; gives him a ministry from heaven; commands him to go and baptize all those who, confessing their sins and professing repentance of them, should come to him.' (*Works*, vol. 6, p. 465)

Mark tells us that 'John did baptize in the wilderness, and preach the baptism of repentance for the remission of sins' (Mark 1:4). John Erskine, whom William Cunningham called 'probably the greatest divine in the Church of Scotland in the latter part of the eighteenth century', remarks:

'John's baptism was termed the baptism of repentance, and baptism to repentance, because he required of all whom he admitted to baptism, a profession of repentance.' *(Theological Dissertations, p. 79.)*

A second witness from Scotland is Thomas Boston:

> 'Acts 14:4 "John verily baptized with the baptism of repentance" not in respect of repentance to come after, but going before; for John baptized none but those that confessed their sins, Matthew 3:6' (*Works*, p. 384.)

Among the multitudes who came to John's baptism were many of the Pharisees and Sadducees whom John warned saying, 'Think not to say within yourselves, we have Abraham to our father' (Matthew 3:9). It was as if he said, 'You might be the children of the covenant made with Abraham and thereby entitled to circumcision and the Passover irrespective of your moral character, but do not think that any hereditary right qualifies you for my baptism. My baptism is a baptism of *repentance*. Bring forth therefore fruits meet for repentance.' Philip Doddridge comments:

> 'Upon this, many of the Pharisees and Sadducees, who expected to have been treated with great respect, were so provoked that they turned their backs upon the prophet, and refused to be baptized. Compare Luke 7:29,30; and Matthew 21:25.' (*Paraphrase* on Luke 3:10.)

John, then, only baptized those who repented of and confessed their sins. Hence, as Thomas Scott comments:

> 'It does not appear that any but adults were baptized by him.' (*Commentary* on Matthew 3:5,6.)

There is therefore no evidence that John baptized babies. In fact, the evidence is against it, because had John baptized babies, his baptism could hardly have been called the baptism of repentance. Nor is it easy to understand how the baptizing of babies would have fitted in with the purpose of his mission, namely, to prepare people for the coming of the King and the kingdom.

We can sum up in the words of that 'earnest champion of the strictest orthodoxy of the canons of Dort' Francis Turretine:

> 'John admitted none to baptism but those who confessed their sins; because his business was to baptize adults.' (*Institutes of Theology*, section 4, question 22.)

Chapter 3
Did Christ baptize babies?

From John 3:22,26 and John 4:2, it appears that for most, if not all, of his ministry, Jesus deputed the actual work of baptizing converts to his disciples. We are to bear this in mind when in John 4:1 we read that 'Jesus made and baptized disciples'. This statement is very instructive; in particular it teaches us three things:

(1) Those baptized are called disciples
(2) Jesus makes disciples before he baptizes them
(3) Baptism does not make a disciple

Ralph Wardlaw, the eminent Congregationalist, agrees:

'We have before adverted to the terms of the evangelist, that "Jesus made and baptized more disciples than John;" terms according to which they were not made by disciples by baptism, but made and then baptized.' (*Dissertation on Baptism,* p. 331.)

On John 3:22 Thomas Scott comments:

'Christian baptism "into the name of the Father, and of the Son, and of the Holy Ghost", was at this times not instituted … The baptism of Jesus was doubtless of adults alone.'

Evidence that it was not Christ's custom to baptize babies is found in the way the disciples behaved when babies were brought to him to be blessed (Matthew 19:13-15; Mark 10:13-16; Luke 18:15-17). Had the disciples been accustomed to seeing babies baptized (or rather to baptizing them themselves) they would never have hindered their being brought to their Master. William Burkitt comments:

'They were brought to Christ: but for what end? Not to baptize them, but to bless them .... Christian baptism was not instituted. John's baptism was the baptism of repentance, of which babies were incapable.'

Another Puritan annotator, Matthew Poole, comments:

'We must take heed we do not found infant baptism upon the example of Christ in this text; for it is certain that he did not baptize these children.' (On Matthew 19:14.)

But alas! Poole's warning was given in vain, for scores of Paedobaptists from the Puritans onward (not to mention the Fathers and Reformers before him) have appealed to this incident. Of these J.C.Ryle is one:

'A direct argument in favour of infant baptism the passage certainly is not. But a stronger indirect testimony it seems impossible to conceive.' (*Knots Untied,* p. 100.)

This is one of Ryle's four *reasons* for baby baptism. Again, there is the Prayer Book Service of Infant Baptism in which the only Scripture read is the account of Christ's blessing the children. Apparently the English Reformers also regarded this incident as sanctioning, or at least favouring, the baptism of babies.

Other Paedobaptist writers, however, have been more discriminating. For example, Alfred Plummer writes:

'That little children may be brought to Christ, and are a type of Christian innocence, does not prove that they are fit to receive baptism.' (*Hastings Dictionary of the Bible.*)

B.B Warfield is so sure as to state:

> 'Nobody supposes that Jesus and his disciples were in the
> habit of baptizing infants.' (*Studies in Theology*, p. 399.)

That so many should have appealed to Christ's blessing the children
as proof for baby baptism is indicative of the absence of stronger
proof. Bishop Jeremy Taylor states the matter thus:

> 'From the action of Christ's blessing infants, to infer they are
> to be baptized, proves nothing so much as that there is a want
> of better argument. The conclusion would be with probability
> derived thus:— Christ blessed infants, and so dismissed
> them, but baptized them not; therefore infants are not to be
> baptized.' (*Liberty of Prophesying,* p. 327.)

Let us mark this well. The Lord did not use this occasion as well he
might, had he wanted to institute the baptism of babies. Up to this
time he had not ordered his disciples to baptize babies. If therefore
it was his will that henceforth babies should be baptized, what better
occasion than this to say so? Why should he not give his disciples
a lesson by baptizing these babies there and then? Or why not
explicitly order his disciples that in future babies were to be baptized
— especially as he had just taught them. 'Of such is the kingdom of
heaven?'

Perhaps some will say that these words provide a warrant for the
baptism of babies. But if this were the case, why did not the disciples
go and baptize these children? Or was it that Christ's words were not
plain enough? Professor John Murray is undoubtedly correct when
he writes:

> 'These two assertions — (1) that little children belong to the
> kingdom of God; (2) that they are to be received in Christ's
> name — do not offer stringent proof of infant baptism and
> they do not provide us with an express command to baptize
> infants.' (*Christian Baptism,* p. 65.)

So, whatever the meaning of the words 'of such is the kingdom of
heaven', the fact that these children were not baptized indicates, if
anything, that babies are not to be baptized.

One last point. If any ceremony is sanctioned by the action of Christ's blessing the children, it is not the baptizing of babies but baby blessing. (See Appendix A for the order of service.)

Chapter 4
Did Christ order the baptism of babies?

If there is any place where we can expect to find the mind of the Lord concerning the proper subjects of baptism, it is his commission to baptize, recorded in Matthew 28:18-20 and Mark 16:15,16. Since these are the only instructions regarding baptism given us in the whole of Scripture, they are worthy of the closest scrutiny. Like the passages containing the institution of the Lord's Supper, these words have been the occasion of countless controversies.

A common interpretation of Christ's commission to baptize is that given by Philip Schaff:

> 'When the Lord, after solemnly declaring that all power is given to him in heaven and in earth, commands his apostles to make all nations disciples [mathéteuein] by baptism in the triune Name and by the instruction in His doctrine, there is not the least reason for limiting this to those of maturer age. Or do the nations consist only of men, and not of youth also, and children?' (*History of the Apostolic Church*, vol. 2, p. 261.)

This is plausible enough until we look more closely at the wording of this commission: 'Go ye therefore, and teach (mathéteusate, literally, disciple, or make disciples of) all nations, baptizing them in (eis or into) the name of the Father, and of the Son, and of the Holy Ghost: teaching (didaskontes) them to observe all things whatsoever I have commanded you.'

Richard Baxter observes:

> 'This is not like some occasional historical mention of baptism, but it is the very commission of Christ to his apostles for preaching and baptism, and purposely expresseth their several works in their several places and order. Their first task is by teaching to make disciples, which are by Mark called believers. The second work is to baptize them...The third work is to teach them all other things, which are afterwards to be learned in the school of Christ. To contemn this order is to renounce all rules of order; for where can we expect to find it if not here?' (*Disputations of Right to Sacrament*, p. 149f.)

Notwithstanding, Baxter's Puritan contemporary, Thomas Watson, is quite happy to contemn this order, when he writes:

> 'In a heathen nation, first teach them, and then baptize them; but in a Christian church, first baptize them, and then teach them.' (*The Ten Commandments*, p. 160.)

Another one to admit the fact, but not the consequence, of the order expressed in Christ's commission to baptize is James Bannerman, who writes:

> 'The apostolic commission in Mark is to this effect: "Go ye into all the world and preach the Gospel to every creature. He that believeth, and is baptized, shall be saved; he that believeth not shall be damned." It is abundantly obvious that this language applies primarily to the ordinary case of adults, and not to the exceptional case of infants, and while the order — first belief, and then Baptism — refers to adults, it cannot apply to infants, to whom the Gospel cannot be preached, and who cannot be expected to believe it.' (*The Church of Christ*, vol. 2, p. 104f.)

Seeing that the order is so plain, it is small wonder that the Roman Catholic Bishop Bossuet taunts the Reformed Churches, writing:

> 'Jesus Christ has said, "Teach and baptize", and again, "He that believeth and is baptized shall be saved." But the church,

solely by the authority of tradition and custom, has so interpreted these words, that the instruction and faith which Christ had joined with baptism might be separated from it in the case of infants. These words, "Teach and baptize', have a long time perplexed our Reformed gentleman.' (*On the Holy Supper*, p. 127f.)

They still do!
So important is this commission to baptize, that space will be given to several more questions:

John Calvin: 'Christ enjoins that those who have submitted to the gospel, and professed to be his disciples, shall be baptized; partly that it may be an outward sign of faith b e - fore men.' (*Harmony of the Evangelists*, vol. 3 p. 385.)

Charles Simeon: '1. They were to teach all nations. 2. They were to baptize their converts in the name of the sacred three.' (*Expository Outlines in loc.*)

David Brown: 'Set the seal of visible discipleship upon the converts by baptizing them.' (*Jamieson, Fausset and Brown Commentary — unabridged.*)

Louis Berkhof: 'They who accepted Christ by faith were to be baptized in the name of the triune God, as a sign and seal of the fact that they had entered into a new relation to God and as such were obliged to live according to the laws of the kingdom of God.' (*Systematic Theology*, p. 642.)

The commission leads Calvin to call baptism 'partly an outward sign of faith.' Is this the case when babies are baptized? Obviously not, because as Professor John Murray says of babies:

'They are not psychologically capable of such faith and its corresponding confession.' (*Christian Baptism* p. 74.)

Brown calls baptism 'the sign of visible discipleship'. Is baptism such to babies? Can babies be called disciples or learners? W.H. Griffith Thomas writes:

'The great commission of our Lord was. "Go ye and make disciples of all nations. baptizing them .... teaching them", and as the term "disciple" means a "learner", it is obvious that children are rightly included under this description.' (*The Catholic Faith*, p. 395.)

Of course *children* may be learners, but not *babies*. And the famous Genevan Professor of Theology, Francis Turretine, agrees; for he writes that babies:

'are no more capable of actual faith than they are of that instruction with which the adults are to be taught and made disciples of Christ, Matthew 28:19.' (*Institutes of Theology*, part 2, section 9.)

Some advocates of paedobaptism are prepared to go to unusual lengths to get babies into our Lord's commission. For example, Edward Bickersteth writes:

'The infants of believing parents are, from their very birth, learners of Christ.' (*On Baptism*, p. 36.)

J. Lange, the German commentator, goes even further, when on Matthew 28:19 he writes:

'To make disciples of, involves, in general, it is true, the preaching of the gospel; but it marks pre-eminently the moment the non-Christian is brought to a full willingness to become a Christian.'

And later on he writes:

'This willingness in the case of the children of Christian parents is pre-supposed in the willingness of the parents.'

So, we are told, babies are learners, willing learners, from their very birth! We wonder how many parents, speaking from experience, will agree that this is indeed the case with their baptized offspring. That our Lord's words have only to do with those capable of faith and discipleship is a fact conceded by John Calvin. On this commission he writes:

'As Christ enjoins them to teach before baptizing, and d e - sires that none but believers shall be admitted to baptism, it would appear that baptism is not properly administered unless when it is preceded by faith.' (*Harmony of the Gospels,* vol.3, p. 386)

Then on Acts 8:26 Calvin writes:

'Baptism is, as it were, an appurtenance of faith, and therefore it is later in order; secondly, if it be given without faith whose seal it is, it is both a wicked and also a too gross a profanation.' (*Commentary on Acts,* vol.1, p. 362)

In both places Calvin goes on to state that the concessions yield nothing to Baptists, but whether they do or not, the reader can judge for himself. Is not A.Plummer right when he says:

'Make disciples of all nations' (Matthew 28:19) implies those who are old enough to receive instruction.' (*Hastings Bible Dictionary.*)

That this commission gives no direction regarding the baptism of babies is conceded by Dr. Wall, the famous author of a very learned and voluminous history of the baptism of babies, who writes:

'The commission given by our Saviour to his disciples in the time of his mortal life, to baptize in the country of Judaea, is not at all set down in Scripture; only it is said that they baptized a great many. And the enlargement of that commission among all the heathen nations, is set down in such brief words, that there is no particular direction given what they were to do in reference to the children of those that received the faith.' (*History of Infant Baptism,* vol.1, p. 5.)

Weigh this well. The Lord said nothing about babies.

We have already seen that John did not baptize babies, neither did Christ in the time of his mortal life. This being so, if babies are henceforth to be baptized, we expect some command to this effect. Would the apostles dare to start something new without a 'Thus saith the Lord' to warrant it? But as it is, the commission contains not a word about babies.

J.C.Ryle argues thus:

'The point settled by the text is not so much what ought to be done with the children of Christians, as what ought to be done with heathens when converted.' (*Expository Thoughts on Matthew*, p. 411.)

But if this is Christ's only command to baptize, and it says not a word about babies, the point is settled that they must become disciples before this commission has anything to do with them.

In the light of our examination of Christ's commission, which is the only explicit direction given us regarding the administration of baptism, it is clear that, in the words of Louis Berkhof:

'There is not explicit command in the Bible to baptize children.' (*Systematic Theology,* p. 632.)

Chapter 5
Did the Apostles baptize babies?

In the previous chapter it was seen that the recorded commission of Christ authorises the baptism of disciples or believers, and none else. We expect, therefore, that the apostles, regulating their conduct by their Master's commission, will not be found baptizing babies. However, there is the possibility that at some time or other the apostles received a special revelation from their Lord in heaven commissioning the baptism of babies. And so, if we find the apostles baptizing babies, we must presume that they received some such commission which is not recorded in Scripture. It will be on the basis of this unrecorded commission that the practice of baby baptism will be founded. Now the only way to demonstrate the existence of an unrecorded commission is to argue from the uniform practice of the apostles.

In order to ascertain whether it was the custom of the apostles to baptize babies, we shall examine all the cases of baptism which the Holy Spirit has seen fit to record in Holy Scripture.

1. The baptism of about 3,000
On the day of Pentecost Peter's exhortation to the people was: 'Repent, and be baptized every one of you in the name of Jesus Christ for the remission of sins, and ye shall receive the gift of the Holy Ghost. For the promise is unto you, and to your children, and to all that are afar off, even as many as the Lord our God shall call' (Acts 2:38,39). And what happened? 'Then they that gladly received his word were baptized' (v.41). There is no mention of babies.

But it will be asked, 'How about verse 39? Does not Peter say that the promise is to their *children*?' Dr. R. Wilson, the Belfast Presbyterian Professor, states:

> 'Baptist writers both in earlier and more recent times have felt it difficult to dispose of the children comprehended in this precious promise.' (*Infant Baptism*, p. 304.)

Let us look at this precious promise. We notice that 'the promise is unto ....as many as the Lord our God shall call.' This qualifying clause can be interpreted in two ways. Matthew Henry takes the call to be the Lord's effectual call:

> 'To this general (promise) the following limitation must refer, even as many of them, as many particular persons in each nation, as the Lord our God shall call effectually into the fellowship of Jesus Christ.' (*Commentary in loc.*)

Dr. Wilson, on the other hand, disagrees:

> 'A general gospel-call is the doctrine of the text'. (*Infant Baptism*, p. 509.)

Either way it makes no difference, because babies are incapable of understanding or responding to a call, general or effectual. The limiting clause excludes babies so long as they are babies.

This is more clearly seen when we understand what 'the promise' was. Doddridge explains it thus:

> 'The promise is to you and to your children. Considering that the gift of the Spirit had been mentioned just before, it seems most natural to interpret this as a reference to that passage in Joel which had been so largely cited above, where God promised the effusion of the Spirit on their sons and daughters; and accordingly, I have paraphrased the latter clause of this verse as referring to its extra-ordinary gifts: and the rather as the sanctifying influences of the Spirit must already have been received to prepare them for entering the church by baptism.' (*Paraphrase in loc.*)

Did any baby prophesy? Did any babe dream a dream? Did any suckling see a vision? The promise, then, was not to them.

Albert Barnes comments:

'*To your children..* In Joel, to their sons and daughters, who should, nevertheless, be old enough to prophesy. Similar promises occur in Isaiah 44:3, "I will pour out my Spirit on thy seed, and my blessing on thine offspring" and Isaiah 59:21. In these and similar places their descendants and posterity are denoted. It does not refer to children, and should not be adduced to establish the propriety of infant baptism.' (*Commentary* in loc.)

Dr. Hammond writes to the same effect:

'If any have made use of that very inconcludent argument (Acts 2:39), I have nothing to say in defence of them. I think that the practice is founded on a better basis than so; that the word children there is really the posterity of the Jews, and not their infant children.' (*Works*, vol. 1, p. 490.)

It is interesting that Dr. Hammond was nominated one of the Westminster Assembly of Divines, but never sat among them. Had he done so, he might have prevented them from including Acts 2:38,39 as a proof-text for baby baptism. (See Larger Catechism A. 166.)

2. The baptism of the Samaritans
When the Samaritans 'believed Philip preaching the things concerning the kingdom of God, and the name of Jesus Christ, they were baptized, both men and women' (Acts 7:12). Luke calls attention to the fact that women were baptized, but not a word about babies. Is it not likely he would have added 'and children' if in fact children had been baptized?

3. The baptism of the eunuch
Since Acts 8:37 is generally regarded as spurious, suffice it to remark that the eunuch's joy (v.39) shows that he was a believer.

4. The baptism of Saul
Ananias' words to Saul, as recorded in Acts 22:16, are very significant: 'Arise, and be baptized, and wash away thy sins, calling on the name of the Lord.' Adam Clarke comments:

> 'Let this washing of thy body represent to thee the washing away of thy sins.' (*Commentary* in loc.)

Baptism is the sign of the absolution, or washing away, of the sins of the person baptized. Is it such when babies are baptized? (More on this later.)

5. The baptism of Cornelius and his kinsmen and near friends.
While Peter preached to them, 'the Holy Ghost fell on all of them that heard the word' (Acts 10:44) who 'spake with tongues' (v. 46). Thus, those who were baptized, heard the word (presumably intelligently), and spake with tongues. Again babies would seem to be excluded.

6. The baptism of Lydia and her household (Acts 16:15) J.A. Alexander comments:

> 'Her household, lit. house, supposed by some to mean here her family, by others her assistants in her business. Both being mere conjectures, and entirely compatible with o n e another, there is nothing in the text to decide the controverted question, whether children were baptized on this occasion.' (*Commentary on the Acts of the Apostles* in loc.)

He goes on to say that 'the whole dispute' on this subject 'rests on grounds entirely independent of' the 'mention of whole houses being baptized.' And David Brown agrees:

> 'The question of Infant Baptism must be determined on other grounds,' (Jamieson, Fausset, and Brown.)

This is not surprising, considering that there is no proof that Lydia was even married, let alone had any children.

7. The baptism of the jailer and all his (Acts 16:33.)

It should be sufficient to notice verse 34 where we are informed that the jailer 'rejoiced, believing in God with all his house.' This is an example of a whole family believing. (See also John 4:53.) Were there any babies in this family? If so, it would seem they believed and rejoiced.

The words 'and thy house' in verse 31 are interpreted by some to mean that God saves families rather than individuals. For example, Thomas M'Crie, famous as the biographer of John Knox, argues:

'In his covenant with Noah God included his sons as well as himself. In his covenant with Abraham, he included his children as well as himself .... The same principle is as clearly developed in the New Testament ... Do we then say the promise of salvation was given to the whole household, in virtue of the faith of its head? Certainly not in the same sense. But surely there must be some sense in which it holds true ... God does not, indeed, pledge himself to save very member of the family; but if even one of the family is eventually saved, the promise would be fulfilled, and fulfilled in virtue of the covenant relation into which the house was brought with God.' (*Lectures on Christian Baptism,* p. 53f.)

Matthew Henry argues quite differently:

'Believe, and salvation shall come to thy house, Luke 19:8. Those of thy house that are babies, shall be admitted into the visible church with thee, and thereby put into a fair way of salvation.' (*Commentary* in loc.)

M'Crie and Henry have this in common: each dilutes the meaning of a key word. The former reduces 'house' to possibly one child of the family; the latter reduces 'saved' to 'put into a fair way of salvation.'

Turning to other commentators, we find J.A. Alexander commenting as follows:

'Thou and thy house (or household, see above on v.15) does not mean that they were to be saved by his faith, but by faith in the same Saviour.' (*Commentary* in loc.)

And another American commentator, Albert Barnes, comments:

> 'Salvation was offered to his family as well as himself;
> implying that if they believed they should also be saved.'
> (*Commentary* in loc.)

Further evidence is found in verses 32 and 34 on which Olshausen
comments:

> 'The remark in v.32 that Paul preached not only to the jailer
> but also to all en te oikia, is plainly not favourable to the view,
> that infant children are included under this expression f o r
> Paul could deliver no discourse to them.' (*Commentary* in
> loc.)

8. The baptism of Crispus and other Corinthians
In Acts 18:8 we read: 'And Crispus, the chief ruler of the synagogue,
believed on the Lord with all his house; and many of the Corinthians
hearing believed, and were baptized.' Only believers are said to
have been baptized. Notice, too, we have here another example of
a whole family *believing*.

Another of the converts probably baptized at this time was
Stephanas (1 Corinthians 1:8). In 1 Corinthians 16:15 Paul writes
that 'the house of Stephanas have addicted themselves to the
ministry of the saints' or, as Charles Hodge explains it, 'devoted
themselves to the service of believers.' If there were any babies in
this household, it seems they were devoted to the service of the
saints!

It is scarcely surprising that Neander admits:

> 'We cannot prove that the apostles ordained infant baptism
> from these places, where the baptism of a whole family is
> mentioned.' (*Church History*, vol. 1, p. 430.)

The same admission is made by a contemporary Paedobaptist.
Pierre Marcel (and the italics are his):

> 'We state here with all desirable precision that these passages
> have never served and still do not serve, in *good* Reformed

theology, as a *basis or justification* of infant baptism.' (*The Biblical Doctrine of Infant Baptism.* p. 196.)

In the light of this statement, contrast the reasoning of James Bannerman:

'The repeated mention of household or family baptism is of itself decisive evidence of the practice by which babies were baptized.' (*Church of Christ*, vol. 2, p. 93.)

9. The baptism of about twelve men at Ephesus (Acts 19:1-7)
Those baptized in the name of the Lord Jesus are called 'certain disciples' (v.1) 'baptized with the baptism of repentance' (v.4). In verse 6 we read that 'they spake with tongues and prophesied'. Such terms seem to preclude babies from the number baptized.

Having reviewed every case of apostolic baptism on record, we understand why Professor John Murray has to admit that

'We do not have an overt and proven instance of infant baptism.' (Christian Baptism, p. 69.)

Thomas Boston makes the same admission:

'There is no example of baptism recorded in the Scriptures, where any were baptized, but such as appeared to have a saving interest in Christ.' (*Works*, p. 384.)

This fact is made use of by Richard Baxter when discussing the nature of faith, the profession of which gives one a right to baptism. He issues a challenge to his opponent in no uncertain fashion:

'I conclude that all examples of Baptism in Scripture do mention only the administration of it to the professors of saving faith; and the precepts give us no other direction. And I provoke Mr. Blake, as far as it is seemly for me to do, to name one precept or example for baptizing any other, a n d make it good if he can.' (*Disputation of Right to Sacrament,* p. 156.)

Thus, it is established that, in the words of Louis Berkhof,

'The New Testament contains no direct evidence for the practice of infant baptism in the days of the apostles.' (*Systematic Theology*, p. 634.)

Chapter 6
Indirect Evidence

Seeing that there is no *direct* evidence for the practice of baby baptism in the days of the apostles, we now have to assess the *indirect* evidence. To do this, we must first look at those texts which are commonly adduced as inferring the existence of the baptism of babies in the apostolic church,

1. 1 Corinthians 7:14, 'For the unbelieving husband is sanctified by the wife, and the unbelieving wife is sanctified by the husband: else were your children unclean, but now they are holy.' The Paedobaptist argument runs thus: the children of Christians are holy in the same sense in which the children of the Jews were holy. 'Holy' means that they are members of God's community; therefore they are entitled to the membership badge, which was circumcision in the Jewish community, and baptism in the Christian community.

It is interesting to observe that the inference of Christian Paedobaptists is the very opposite of that of the Jewish rabbis. On page ... we saw how they argued that children born in holiness do not require to be baptized.

Thomas Scott comments on 1 Corinthians 7:14 thus:

'I cannot but conclude, after long attention to the subject, that the baptism of the infant-offspring of Christians is here evidently referred to, as at that time customary in the churches.' (*Commentary* in loc.)

But B.B. Warfield is not so sure. In fact, he admits that this verse is:

'no doubt capable of an interpretation on the supposition that that practice did not exist and is scarcely a sure foundation concerning it.' (*Studies in Theology*, p. 398.)

The interpretation of 1 Corinthians 7:14 turns on the meaning of the words 'holy' (hagios) and 'sanctified' (hagiazò), words which have more than one meaning in Scripture. Which meaning the words have here is to be determined by the text and context.

Whatever the apostle intends by the term holy as here applied to children one of whose parents is a believer, it is not confined to the babies of such persons, but belongs to all their offspring, whether younger or older, whether born before the conversion of either parents, or after that happy event had taken place; for the children, without any distinction, are pronounced holy. If, therefore, it is lawful to baptize them on the ground of this holiness while babies, it must be equally so when grown up. Moreover, the holiness of the children is not inferred from the faith of the unbelieving parent, but from the sanctification of the unbelieving party, by or to the believer. Whence it follows that the holiness of the children cannot be superior, either as to nature or degree, to that sanctification of the unbelieving partner from which it is derived.

Now what holiness or sanctification has an unbeliever? Certainly not the sanctification of the Spirit, because this is accompanied by the belief of the truth (2 Thessalonians 2:13). Dr. R.Wilson of Belfast states that :

'The holiness predicted of the children is plainly federal holiness.' (*Infant Baptism*, p. 516.)

It is this 'federal holiness' which is supposed to entitle a believer's children to baptism. This would be quite plausible but for the apostle stating that the unbelieving parent is 'sanctified' i.e. possesses 'federal holiness' according to this interpretation. In other words, the unbelieving adult is entitled to baptism!

Against the 'federal holiness' interpretation Albert Barnes writes:

'This passage has often been interpreted, and is often a d - duced to prove that children are 'federally holy', and that they are entitled to the privileges of baptism on the ground of the faith of one of the parents. But against this interpretation there are insuperable objections.

(1) The phrase 'federally holy' is unintelligible, and conveys no idea to the great mass of men. It occurs nowhere in the Scriptures, and what can be meant by it?

(2) It does not accord with the scope and design of the argument. There is not one word about baptism here; not one allusion to it; nor does the argument in the remotest degree bear upon it. The question was not whether children should be baptized, but it was whether there should be separation between man and wife, where one was a Christian and the other was not.

(3) The supposition that this means that the children would be regarded as *illegitimate* if such a separation should take place, is one that accords with the whole scope and design of the argument.

(4) This accords with the meaning of the word 'unclean'. (He quotes Acts 10:28. See the rest of his comments on this verse.])

Barnes is by no means the only Paedobaptist to hold this view. Another is Wolfius:

'The generality of our Lutheran divines understand the sanctification of the unbelieving partner only in this sense: Paul asserts that a marriage of this kind ought to be esteemed lawful and firm by Christians, though only one of the parties professes the name of Christ.' (Quoted in Booth's *'Paedobaptists Examined'*.)

That this is the interpretation most likely to be correct is clear from the context. The first word of verse 14, 'for', shows that our verse is intended to supply a reason why a believer should not leave or divorce his or her unbelieving partner. The Christians at Corinth were undoubtedly familiar with the teaching of the Jewish Rabbis that 'he that espouses a Gentile woman, or a servant, they are not espousals' and 'a son begotten of a Gentile woman is no son.' (For references see John Gill in loc.) Furthermore, they would be aquainted with Nehemiah 13:23-27 and Ezra 10:17 from which they might deduce that a 'mixed' marriage was unclean in God's eyes, so that a Christian ought to divorce or leave his or her unbelieving partner. It was to counter such ideas that Paul writes as he does in verse 14. If a Christian finds himself married to an unbeliever, he must remember that his marriage is still clean in God's sight, i.e. acceptable, so that he is not to leave his wife. (See verses 12 and 13.)

In view of the fact that this verse is capable of an interpretation on the supposition that baby baptism was not practised, we cannot but admire the candour of Albert Barnes when he writes:

> 'I believe infant baptism to be proper and right, and an inestimable privilege to parents and children. But a good cause should not be made to rest on feeble supports, nor on forced and unnatural interpretations of the Scriptures. And such I regard the usual interpretation placed on this passage.'

One last point concerning this verse. A few commentators see in 1 Corinthians 7:14 evidence that baptizing babies was *not* practised at the time Paul wrote his first epistle to the Corinthians. Dr. Stier writes:

> 'This much on the one hand is true — if infant baptism had been at that time already a universal practice, St. Paul could not have spoken thus paraphrastically concerning it.' (*Words of Jesus*, vol. 8, p. 329.)

Another German commentator, Olshausen, writes:

> 'It is moreover clear that St. Paul could not have chosen this line of argument, had infant baptism been at that time practised.' (*Commentary* in loc.)

Without necessarily agreeing with these German commentators, it is nevertheless remarkable to find that the very text some urge in favour of baptizing babies others regard as evidence against it.

2. Colossians 2:11,12: 'In whom also ye are circumcised with the circumcision made without hands, in putting off the body of the sins of the flesh by the circumcision of Christ: Buried with him in baptism, wherein also ye are risen with him through the faith of the operation of God, who hath raised him from the dead.' The fact that

circumcision and baptism are here linked together shows, it is said, that baptism is the New Testament parallel to circumcision. In short, baptism has come in place of circumcision.

The first thing for us to notice is that Paul does not mention the ordinance of circumcision as such. The circumcision he refers to is 'made without hands' i.e. it is a spiritual circumcision, and that which is put off is not the foreskin but 'the body of the sins of the flesh.' Paul is saying in effect:

> 'Gentile Christians have no need of the rite of circumcision, for they have received from Christ spiritual circumcision of which that rite was the type.' (H.M. Carson in loc.)

Let it be noted that Paul does not argue that Gentile Christians have no need of circumcision because they have been baptized. That which has come in the place of bodily circumcision (the shadow) is spiritual circumcision (the substance), not baptism.

When is this spiritual circumcision effected? Obviously at conversion, when the believer professes to put off the old man, i.e. he repudiates his old nature. It is this thought which naturally leads the apostle to speak of baptism. As H.M. Carson writes:

> 'The putting away of the old nature was openly declared in Christian baptism, which is the visible convenant-seal of the new Israel, just as circumcision was of the old. The picture of being buried beneath the water and rising again is a vivid portrayal of the same truth as that which circumcision has been declaring; for the old man is buried before the new man may rise.' (Op. cit. in loc.)

What Paul is saying is that circumcision and baptism are different symbols of the same truth. But he does not say that baptism has superseded circumcision.

That the apostle Paul did not teach that baptism has come in the place of circumcision is evident from the fact that we find the Christians at Jerusalem still zealous for circumcision in the year AD 60. On the statement 'they are all zealous for the law' in Acts 21:20, Albert Barnes makes the following judicious remarks:

'They still observe the law of Moses. The reference here is to the law respecting circumcision, sacrifices, distinctions of meats and days, festivals, etc. It may seem remarkable that they should still continue to observe those rights, since it was the manifest design of Christians to abolish them. But we are to remember,

(1) That those rites had been appointed by God, and that they were trained to their observance.

(2) That the apostles conformed to them while they remained at Jerusalem and did not deem it best to set themselves violently against them, ch. 3:1, Luke 24:53.

(3) That the question about their observance had never been agitated at Jerusalem. It was only among the Gentile converts that the question had arisen, and there it must arise, for if they were to be observed, they must have been imposed upon them by authority.

(4) The decision of the council (ch. 15) related only to the Gentile converts. It did not touch the question whether those rites were to be observed by the Jewish converts.' (*Commentary on Acts* 21:20.)

Thus, the Christians at Jerusalem continued to circumcise their children. This fact in and of itself shows that baptism was not regarded as having replaced circumcision.

On the supposition that baby baptism was instituted and practised by the apostles, it is remarkable that we never find them teaching: 'Circumcision is out-of-date. Baptism has taken its place. In future, instead of circumcising your children, baptize them.' How easily they might have answered the Judaizers!

It is of course possible that the Jewish Christians had their children both circumcised and baptized, but this is not likely; for why have two ordinances to signify the same spiritual truth? And so the continued practice of circumcision in the church at Jerusalem is strong presumptive evidence that the members of that church did not have their babies baptized. This means that neither Christ nor his apostles could have instituted baptism of babies as obligatory.

Having examined the texts adduced as evidence of the existence of baby baptism in the time of the apostles, we come to the conclusion that

'Not only is there no mention of the baptism of infants, but there is no text from which such baptism can be securely inferred. (A.Plummer in *Hastings Dictionary of the Bible.*)

Let the reader draw his own conclusions.

Chapter 7
Baptism of babies unauthorized by the New Testament

Our findings thus far can be summed up in the words of B.B. Warfield.

> 'It is true that there is no express command to baptize infants in the New Testament, no express record of the baptism of infants, and no passages so stringently implying it that we must infer from them that infants were baptized.' (*Studies in Theology,* p. 399.)

Granted these facts, it logically follows that baby baptism is not authorized by the New Testament. Warfield admits the logicality of this inference when he goes on to write:

> 'The warrant for infant baptism is not to be sought in the New Testament but in the Old Testament.' (p. 399.)

For the present we will overlook his reference to the Old Testament to find a warrant for what is essentially a New Testament ordinance. The arguments from the Old Testament will be considered later. That which demands our immediate attention is this: the warrant for baptizing babies is not to be sought in the New Testament. In making this statement Warfield implies that most of the Patristic and Protestant theologians before him were in error when seeking a warrant for baby baptism in the New Testament.

Warfield is not the only one to admit that baby baptism is without precept and without precedent. Professor John Murray writes:

'It is only too apparent that if we had an express command or even a proven case with apostolic sanction, then the controversy would not have risen; or at least it would be of a very different sort.' (*Christian Baptism*, p. 72.)

The implication is that something may be Scriptural which is without precept or precedent.

When disputing about other matters it is the custom of Reformed Paedobaptists to demand either a precept or a precedent to prove a matter Scriptural. For example, Matthew Poole argues against the indiscriminate baptism of adults thus:

'I cannot be of their mind who think that persons may be baptized before they be taught: we want precedents of any such baptism in Scripture.' (*Annotations* on Matthew 28:19.)

What Poole says of indiscriminate baptism, we say of baby baptism! Another one to argue against indiscriminate baptism is James Bannerman:

'The theory of indiscriminate baptism we set aside as i n - consistent with the nature and meaning of the Sacrament — as destitute of any countenance from the practice of John the Baptist — as contrary to the terms of the apostolic commission, and opposed to the practice of the apostles and the New Testament Church.' (*Church of Christ*, vol. 2, p. 66.)

Bannerman evidently thinks these sufficient grounds upon which to reject indiscriminate baptism. On precisely the same grounds we reject the baptizing of babies!

Using this very same argument, John Owen writes against an 'enthusiastic affection for Christ' as follows:

'It is in no way directed, warranted, approved by any command, promise, or rule of Scripture. As it is without precedent, so it is without precept; and hereby, whether we will or no, all our graces and duties must be tried, as unto any acceptation with God. Whatever pretends to exceed the direction of the word, may be safely rejected, cannot safely be admitted.' (*On the Person of Christ*, p. 170.)

So argue the Reformed in ninety-nine cases out of a hundred. Why make an exception in the case of baby baptism?

As a challenge to all Paedobaptists of the Reformed school, the words of Richard Baxter, concerning another matter, come with his customary vigour:

> 'What man dare go in a way which hath neither precept nor example to warrant it, from a way that hath full current of both? .... Who knows what will please God but himself? And hath he not told us what he expecteth from us? Can that be obedience which hath no command for it? .... O the pride of man's heart, that instead of being true worshippers, they will be worship-makers! .... For my part, I will not fear that God will be angry with me for doing no more than he hath commanded me, and for sticking close to the rule of his word in matter of worship; but I should tremble to add or diminish.' (*Plain Scripture Proof*, pp. 24, 303.)

To escape from this corner some will perhaps argue, is it not possible that the apostles baptized babies without the Holy Spirit recording it in Scripture? The answer to this argument from silence is found in Hebrews 7:14 where the writer shows how we are to argue from silence in the matter of ecclesiastical regulations. The writer is seeking to prove that Christ's priesthood is not after the order of Aaron, in course of which he says: 'And our Lord sprang out of Judah, of which tribe Moses spake nothing concerning the priesthood.' On this verse John Owen comments:

> 'This silence of Moses in this matter, the apostle takes to be a sufficient argument to prove that the legal priesthood did not belong, nor could be transferred, unto the tribe of Judah. And the grounds hereof are resolved into this general maxim: That whatever is not revealed and appointed in the worship of God, by God himself, is to be considered as nothing, yea, as that which is to be rejected. And such he conceived to be the evidence of this maxim, that he chose rather to argue from the silence of Moses in general, than from the particular prohibition, that none, who was not of the posterity of Aaron, should approach unto the priestly office. So God himself condemneth some instances of false worship on this ground.

That he never appointed them; that they never came into his heart; and thence aggravated the sins of the people, rather than from the particular prohibition of them (Jeremiah 7:31).' (*Commentary on Hebrews 7:14.*)

The silence of Scripture concerning baby baptism condemns the practice far more than a particular prohibition of it would!

The stock answer of Paedobaptists when challenged to produce a precept or precedent for the baptism of babies is, 'Give us a precept or precedent for the admission of women to the Lord's Supper.' The only way to justify female communion, it is said, is by inference from Scripture, and it is even thus that baby baptism is established.

The force and relevance of this counter-argument we will now investigate.

First, let us see whether there is any precept that women should partake of the Lord's Supper. The law of institution reads: 'Jesus took bread, and blessed it, and brake it, and gave it to the disciples, and said, Take, eat' (Matthew 26:26-28). The term disciple is the only word in this law by which the subjects of the ordinances are described. Is it not evident that the term disciples applies to women as well as to men (though not to babies, otherwise this would enjoin baby communion!) Believing females are as much disciples as believing males, so that they are under an express command respecting the Lord's Supper.

If it is objected that when the Lord gave this command, there were no females present, we answer that Paul, when recording what he had received from the Lord concerning the Holy Supper, applies, in the most direct manner, the law of institution to the members in general of the church at Corinth (1 Corinthians 11:23-27), and that there were females among them, we are expressly informed (1 Corinthians 14:34,35).

Suppose someone were to ask for a precept or precedent to authorize the admission of Americans to the Lord's Supper. Suppose it were argued that the original law of institution was given to the Jews, and that all the examples in the New testament are of men who were Romans subjects. How would we set about providing the necessary warrant? Would we not argue that the nationality of the communicant is a mere circumstance and that the only real and substantial qualification for communion is that the person be a professed believer. In like manner we can say that the sex of a communicant is a mere circumstance. John Owen writes:

> 'It is merely from a spirit of contention, that some call on us, or others, to produce express testimony or institution for every circumstance in the practice of religious duties in the church; and on a supposed failure herein, to conclude, that they have power themselves to institute and ordain such ceremonies as they think meet, under pretence of their b e - ing circumstances of worship.' (*Enquiry into the Original Nature of Churches*, p. 125.)

Now apply this to baptism. The sex of the party baptized, whether baptism be administered indoors or outdoors, etc., are mere circumstances. The only general rule to be followed is Christ's commission to his apostles, which stipulates, as we have seen, that baptism be administered to professing believers, which rule is violated when administered to babies.

Nor is this all. The whole meaning and significance of baptism is altered when given to babies, as will be seen in a subsequent chapter. But no alteration in the nature or purpose of the Lord's Supper is necessitated when women are allowed to sit down at the Lord's Table.

Explaining why the Reformed Churches do not practice baby communion, Professor John Murray writes:

> 'The notions associated with the Lord's Supper, such as remembrance, communion, discerning of the Lord's body, are of such a nature that they involve conscious intelligent understanding.' (*Christian Baptism*, p. 78.)

In the same manner it can be said that the notions associated with baptism, such as repentance, union with Christ in his death and resurrection, are of such a nature that they involve conscious intelligent understanding. Hence, baptism is not for babies.

Chapter 8
Infant baptism inconsistent with N.T. teaching

In our examination of the Acts of the Apostles we found no proven instance of the apostles baptizing babies. We now turn to the Epistles, in particular to five texts which, it is maintained, could scarcely have been written had the apostles baptized the babies of their converts. Even more important, these texts will demonstrate the inconsistency of baby baptism with the New Testament teaching. We shall see that the apostolic doctrine of baptism has to be modified in order to accommodate babies. As W.H. Griffith Thomas writes:

'It should ever be borne in mind that the language of the New Testament, which describes the blessings associated and pledged in baptism, refers to adults and not to unconscious children, and it is only by necessary accommodation and modification that we can use the same language of the latter.' (*The Catholic Faith*, p. 288.)

Notice the word *necessary*. The language of the New Testament with regard to baptism, as it stands, cannot apply to the ordinance when administered to babies. And the same is true of the Westminster Confession of Faith, the language of which must be modified in the case of babies. (See Appendix C.)

Let us now turn to the five texts in order to establish the charge of inconsistency.

1. Romans 6:2-4

Whatever these verses may teach regarding the mode of baptism, it
is clear to James Bannerman that :

> 'The apostle must be had as referring to the baptism of a
> believer, in whose case it was a spiritual act of faith,
> embodying it in the outward ordinance.' (*Church of Christ,*
> vol. 2, p. 47.)

It is impossible to understand these verses except on the supposition
that all those to whom Paul was writing had been baptized as
professed believers. Charles Hodge's comments on these verses are
very instructive:

> 'Baptism was the appointed mode of professing faith in
> Christ, of avowing allegiance to him as the Son of God, and
> acquiescence in his gospel. Those, therefore, who were
> baptized, are assumed to believe what they professed, a n d
> to be what they declared themselves to be ... When a man
> was baptized unto Christ, he was baptized unto his death; he
> professed to regard himself as being united to   Christ, as
> dying when he died, as bearing in him thepenalty of sin, in
> order that he might be reconciled to God, and live unto ho-
> liness. How could a man who was sincerein receiving bap-
> tism, such being its design and import, live in sin? The thing
> is impossible. The act of faith implied and expressed in
> baptism, is receiving Christ as our sanctification as well as
> our righteousness.' (*Commentary*   in loc.)

Now can this be said of those baptized as babies? Would not Paul
have referred back to their 'confirmation' or some suchlike public
profession of faith? We must remember that the church at Rome to
which Paul was writing was probably not less than twenty-five years
old, so that if baby baptism had been practised, a good proportion of
the church had been baptized as babies. As Doddridge remarks:

> 'The apostles, when writing to Christian churches, planted
> many years before the date of their respective epistles, argue
> with the members of them from the obligation which their
> baptism brought upon them, in such a manner as would lead

us to conclude that they were baptized in their own persons.'
(*Miscellaneous Works*, p. 489f.)

Another witness to the same point is Jonathan Edwards who, in his
'Enquiry into Qualifications for Full Communion', writes:

'Baptism, by which the primitive converts were admitted into
the church, was used as an exhibition of their being visibly
regenerated, dead to sin — as is evident by Romans 6
throughout. He does not mean only that their baptism laid
them under special obligation to these things, and was a mark
and token of their engagement to be thus hereafter; but was
designed as a mark, token and exhibition of their being thus
already.' (*Works*, vol.1, p. 440)

Are babies baptized as 'an exhibition of their being visibly
regenerated'? Where is the Evangelical Protestant who can answer
yes?

2. 1 Corinthians 1:13
What does it mean to be baptized in the name of some one? A.A.
Hodge explains it thus:

'To be baptized "in the name of Paul" (eis to onoma), 1
Corinthians 1:13, or "unto Moses" (eis ton Mousen), 1
Corinthians 10:2, is, on the part of the baptized, to be made
the believing and obedient disciples of Paul or Moses, and the
objects of their care. and the participants in whatever
blessings they had to bestow.' (*Outlines of Theology,* p. 486.)

When babies are baptized into the name of Christ, does it mean that
they are made his 'believing and obedient disciples', etc.? The
meaning of the phrase 'into the name of' makes it impossible for an
baby to be baptized into the name of anyone. He can be baptized *in*
the name, but not *into* the name, of Christ.

George Smeaton, when seeking to prove that divine worship is
to be paid to the Spirit, argues from the nature of baptism thus:

'We have only to consider the nature of the ordinance to
perceive in it a solemn act of worship, an expression of faith,

a testimony that he in whose name it is performed is our God, with a heartfelt surrender to him in an act of new obedience. That all this is involved is clear from the words: "Were ye baptized in the name of Paul?" (1 Corinthians 1:13.)' (*The Doctrine of the Holy Spirit, p. 112f.*)

It is not likely that Smeaton was thinking of babies when he penned these words!

3. Galatians 3:27
This verse is very similar to Romans 6:2-4 as Charles Hodge observes:

'Baptism is throughout this passage (Romans 6:4), as in Galations 3:27, taken for the reception of Christ, of which it is the appointed acknowledgement.' (*Commentary on Romans 6:4.*)

Matthew Henry comments in loc.:

'This faith in Christ whereby they became the children of God, he aquaints us, verse 27, was what they professed in baptism; for he adds, As many of you as have been baptized into Christ, have put on Christ; having in baptism professed their faith in him, they were thereby devoted to him, and had, as it were, put on his livery and declared themselves his servants and disciples.'

Now, can babies put on Christ's livery? Everyone knows that it takes a child several years before he can put on a coat. Had the Galatians been baptized as babies, Paul would have said that they had had Christ put on them!
But it will be said, the Galations churches had not been founded long, so that most of them would have been baptized as believers. Quite true, but notice the words 'as many' on which Dean Alford comments:

'As many as were baptized into Christ, did, in that very act, clothe yourselves with Christ.' (*Greek Testament* in loc.)

Everyone who had been baptized had, in that very act, put on Christ. Since babies cannot put on Christ, we conclude that Paul did not baptize their babies.

4. Colossians 2:12

Linking this verse with Romans 6:4 Dr. Eadie writes:

> 'From these expressions we may infer that the apostle r e - garded baptism as the symbol of a present resurrection from the death of trespasses and sin, to a life of holiness.' (*Biblical Cyclopaedia.*)

Is baby baptism the symbol of the present resurrection of an baby? Arguing against the indiscriminate baptism of adults, Richard Baxter makes his comment on Colossians 2:12:

> 'Note 1. That this is spoken to all the church of the Colossians, and therefore they are presumed to be what they profess and appear to be. 2. That the putting of the body under water did signify our burial with Christ, and the death or putting off of our sins.' (D*isputation of Right to Sacrament*, p. 58.)

He goes on to say that the language supposes 'their own present profession to put off the body of sin and their consent to be baptized on these terms' of profession. His argument against indiscriminate baptism has the same weight against the baptizing of babies. Furthermore, can babies be said to have risen with Christ through the faith of the operation of God?

5. 1 Peter 3:20,21
What are we to understand by the answer of a good conscience? The Westminster Assembly of Divines say:

> 'By the answer of a good conscience we may understand that unfeigned faith whereof they made confession at their baptism.' (*Annotations* in loc.)

Does baptism give a baby a good conscience? If so, how?

How are we to explain the controversial words 'baptism saves'?

Richard Baxter reasons thus:

> 'Baptism is said to save us, and therefore they that will be
> baptized must profess the qualification necessary to be
> saved.' (*Practical Works*, vol. 4, p. 296.)

Hence, baptism is not for babies.

In an attempt to deny this obvious inference, Patrick Fairburn
writes:

> 'And if baptism also is said to save, and is especially
> associated with the work of regeneration — as it undoubtedly
> is — it can only be because baptism is viewed, in the case of
> the adult believer, as the proper consummation and   em-
> bodiment of faith's actings in the reception of Christ.' (*The
> Revelation of Law*, p. 266.)

We see that Fairburn would limit Peter's statement to the case of the
adult believer; but Peter makes no such limitation. Fairburn is
compelled to admit that the ideal baptism, adult baptism, undergoes
'a certain accommodation' in the case of babies. But where is the
authority for this certain accommodation? It is not to be found in
Scripture. It seems to us that Peter would never have stated that
baptism saves, if he had been in the habit of baptizing any except
professed believers.

William Cunningham rightly remarks that:

> 'The texts referred to seem to imply either, that baptism, in
> the right and legitimate use of it, is a sign or symbol, a seal
> and a profession of remission and regeneration, as previously
> and then existing in the party baptized; or else that
> regeneration is produced or bestowed in baptism, and
> through the instrumentality of that ordinance. The first of
> these views is, we are persuaded, that which is sanctioned by
> Scripture, and certainly it has been generally taught by t h e
> Reformed Churches.' (*The Reformers and the Theology of*

the Reformation, p. 271.)

In other words, these texts teach either believers' baptism or baptismal regeneration. Let the reader take his choice.

The reasons for thinking that the apostles regarded baptism as an act of faith on the part of the person baptized, are summed up by Charles Hodge thus:

> 'To baptism may be properly attributed all that in the Scriptures is attributed to faith. Baptism washes away the sin (Acts 22:16); it unites to Christ and makes us sons of God (Galations 3:26,27); we are therein buried with Christ (Romans 6:3); it is (according to one interpretation of Titus 3:5) the washing of regeneration. But all this is said on the assumption that it is what it purports to be, an act of faith.' (*Systematic Theology,* vol. 3, p. 589.)

Is baptism an act of faith in the case of babies? Can we attribute to baby baptism all that which in the Scriptures is attributed to faith? Understanding the doctrine of baptism as held and taught by the apostles, J.V. Bartlett writes:

> 'It is not only that there is no trace of it (infant baptism) in the first century: but the very idea of baptism then universal, namely as a rite of faith's self-consecration (often outwardly ratified by manifestations of the Spirit) is inconsistent therewith.' (*The Apostolic Age,* p. 472.)

Here we have the admission of a Paedobaptist that the apostolic idea of baptism is inconsistent with the baptism of babies.

Writing in the same vein, H.C. McGiffert observes:

> 'Whether infants were baptized in the apostolic age, we have no means of determining. Where the original idea of baptism as a baptism of repentance, or where Paul's profound conception of it as a symbol of death and resurrection of the believer with Christ prevailed, the practice would not be likely to arise. But where the rite was regarded as a mere sign of one's reception into the Christian circle, it would be

possible for the custom to grow up under the influence of the ancient idea of the family as a unit in religion as well as in all other matters.' (*History of Christianity in the Apostolic Age*, p. 543.)

We agree with McGiffert except that it would be more true to say that the custom of baptizing babies grew up under the influence of the idea of baptismal regeneration. But however baby baptism originated, it is clear that it was only when Paul's conception of baptism, that is, when the New Testament conception of baptism, ceased to prevail, that baby baptism could be introduced into the church. And when was the baptism of babies introduced? That is the subject of the next chapter.

Chapter 9
The antiquity of the baptism of babies

Many advocates of baby baptism claim with A.A. Hodge that

> 'The early church, in unbroken continuity from the days of
> the apostles, testify to their custom on this subject.'
> (*Confession of Faith*, p. 348.)

This claim we will now subject to close scrutiny. At the outset it
must be stated that, as Protestants, we follow the Fathers only so far
as they follow Christ and his apostles. The Patristic writings,
interesting as they are, form no part of the divine rule of faith and
practice. To be unduly influenced by the opinions and traditions of
the fathers is to be false to the Reformed position, because:

> 'The Supreme Judge, by which all controversies of religion
> are to be determined, and all decrees of councils, opinions of
> ancient writers, doctrines of men, and private spirits, are to
> be examined, and in whose sentence we are to rest, can be no
> other but the Holy Spirit speaking in the scripture.'
> (*Westminster Confession of Faith*, 1.10.).

So many extravagant statements have been made concerning the
antiquity of baby baptism that it is necessary to itemise the evidence
in order that every reader may judge for himself. The references to
baptism in the first two centuries have been traced from the indices
of the volumes of the Ante-Nicene Christian Library. Several other

passages supposed to have some bearing on the subject will also be considered.

Those authors who were the immediate disciples of the apostles are called 'apostolic Fathers'. Much of that which bears their name is supposed to be spurious, or, being genuine, to be so interpolated, that we can do no more than guess what is really theirs.

The so-called epistle of Barnabas, written about A.D. 125, mentions baptism, but nothing about babies.

The shepherd or pastor of Hermas, written about A.D. 150, teaches that 'the baptism of water is necessary to all.' Doddridge remarks:

> 'The pastor of Hermas is a visionary book, the genuineness of which is far from being certain; but allowing it to have ever so much weight, this will only prove that baptism is necessary to those who are the proper subjects of it; but cannot determine that babies are so.' (*Miscellaneous Works*, p. 493.)

The next so-called apostolic Father is Dionysius who died around A.D. 95. The great authority on the apostolic Fathers, J.B.Lightfoot, writes:

> 'The works of Dionysius the Areopagite are now universally condemned as spurious.' (*Apostolic Fathers*, vol. 1, p. 4.)

Ignatius, who died A.D. 107, was the author of seven or more epistles none of which says anything about baptizing babies.

Clement of Rome, author of a most edifying epistle to the Corinthians, never mentions baptism. Several works have been attributed to Clement, but these Lightfoot rejects as spurious (see *Apostolic Fathers*, vol. 1, p. 100f.). Clement died around A.D. 100.

The apocryphal gospels are so full of nonsense that no one, that is, no Protestant, ever quotes them as evidence of anything, except perhaps of the puerility of their authors, and the credulity of their readers during the Dark Ages.

There is then not the least shred of evidence that baby baptism was known or practised by any of the immediate 'successors' of the apostles. This brings us to about A.D. 130.

Coming to the writings of the period A.D. 130-200, we find no trace of baby baptism in the works of Melito, Polycarp, Theophilus of Antioch, Athenagoras, and Clement of Alexandria. The Didache, thought to belong to this period, speaks of adult, but not of baby baptism.

The first 'possible reference', as Professor G.W. Bromiley calls it (*The Baptism of Infants*, p. 1), is in Justin Martyr who speaks of some men and women sixty and seventy years old, who, (ek paidon emathetéuthesan to christo), from childhood were discipled to Christ. Louis Berkhof concedes that:

> 'Ek paidon does not necessarily mean infancy.' (*Systematic Theology*, p. 635.)

Hence Dr. L. Woods, the first professor of theology at Andover Seminary, concludes:

> 'As the phrase, ek paidon, may relate to children who have come to years of understanding, as well as to babies, I am well satisfied on a review of the testimony of Justin, that it cannot well be urged as conclusive in favour of Paedobaptism.' (*Lectures on Infant Baptism*, p. 112.)

It is providential that elsewhere in his writings Justin gives what Dr. Wall describes as:

> the most ancient account of the way of baptism, next the Scriptures, and shows the plain and simple manner of administering it.' (*History of Infant Baptism,* vol. 1, p. 64.)

This account is so important that we will quote it at length:

> 'As many as are persuaded and believe that what we teach and say is true, and undertake to be able to live accordingly, are instructed to pray and to entreat God with fasting, for the remission of their sins that are past, we   praying and fasting with them. Then they are brought by us to where there is water, and are regenerated in the same manner in which we were ourselves regenerated. For, in the name of God, the Father and Lord of the universe, and of our Saviour Jesus Christ, and of the Holy Spirit. They then receive the washing with water.

And for this (rite) we have learned from the apostles this reason. Since at our birth we were born without our knowledge and choice, by our parents coming together, and were brought up in bad habits and wicked training; in o r - der that we may not remain the children of necessity and of ignorance, but may become the children of choice and knowledge, and may obtain in the water the remission of sins formerly committed, there is pronounced over him who chooses to be born again, and has repented of his sins, the name of God, the Father and Lord of the universe; he who leads to the laver the person to be washed calling him by this name alone ... And this washing is called illumination, because they who learn these things are illuminated in their understandings.' (*Ante-Nicene Christian Library*, vol. 2, p. 59f.)

Here we have from a second century Father a positive testimony against baby baptism; an assertion that the baptism which had been handed down from the apostles was an ordinance in which one was to exercise choice and knowledge. Evidently Justin knew nothing of baby baptism. Justin, it should be noticed, died around A.D. 165. F.J. Foakes-Jackson writes that:

'The testimony of Irenaeus is the earliest direct evidence in favour of baby baptism.' (*History of the Christian Church*, p. 23.)

The passage in Irenaeus reads as follows:

'For he came to save all through means of himself — all I say who through him are born again (regenerated) to God — babies, and children, and boys, and youths, and old men. He therefore passed through every age, becoming a baby f o r babies, thus sanctifying babies; a child for children ... So likewise he became an old man for old men.' (*Ante-Nicene Christian Library, Writings of Irenaeus*, vol. 1, p. 199f.)

It is well-known that the Fathers often call baptism regeneration; hence to be regenerated is to be baptized. As William Cunningham remarks:

'Before the end of the third century, the Fathers were accustomed to speak of baptism as being at once, the remission of sin and the renovation of the moral nature; and though this mode of speaking was originally adopted upon the assumption that the faith which unites men to Christ, and is the instrumental cause of justification, and, in the full sense of the word, of moral renovation, existed, and was expressed or embodied in the reception of baptism, yet this consideration was gradually lost sight of, and they began to talk as if baptism of itself necessarily implied all this.' (*Historical Theology*, vol. 1, p. 203.)

Now while third century authors generally use the term regeneration to mean baptism, it is far from certain that this was the usage in the second century, to which century belongs Irenaeus. On this passage of his, Doddridge remarks:

'We have only a Latin translation of this work; and some critics have supposed the passage spurious; or, allowing it to be genuine, it will not be granted that to be regenerate a l - ways in his writings signifies to be baptized.' (*Miscellaneous Works*, p. 493.)

To the same effect writes Hagenbach in his History of Doctrines:

'The passages from Scripture which are thought to intimate that infant baptism had come into use in the primitive church, are doubtful and prove nothing. Nor does the earliest passage occurring in the writings of the Fathers (Iren. adv. Haer. 2. 22) afford any decisive proof. It only expresses the beautiful idea that Jesus was Redeemer in every stage of life, and for every stage of life, but it does not say that he redeemed children by the water of baptism, unless the term renasci be interpreted by the most petitio principii (i.e. begging the question) to refer to baptism.' (P. 193f.)

It will have been noticed that Irenaeus in this selfsame passage states that Christ became an old man for old men which is manifestly false. Matthew Henry pertinently remarks:

'Irenaeus, one of the first fathers, with this passage (John 8:57) supports the tradition, which he saith he had from some that had conversed with St. John, that our Saviour lived to be fifty years old. See what little credit is to be given to tradition.' (*Commentary* on John 8:57.)

Tertullian, writing about A.D. 200, is the first person in Christian history to mention baby baptism, and it is not a little significant that this author, so tenacious of other apostolic traditions, writes against the practice of baptizing babies. His words are as follows:

'And so, according to the circumstances and disposition, and even age, of each individual, the delay of baptism is preferable; principally, however, in the case of little children ... The Lord does indeed say, "Forbid them not to come unto me." Let them "come', then, while they are growing up; let them"come   while they are learning; let the become Christians when they have become able to know Christ.' (*Works of Tertullian*, p. 253.)

This extract leads Neander to remark:

'In the last years of the second century Tertullian appears as a zealous opponent of baby baptism.' (*Church History*, vol. 1, p. 425.)

Now what can we conclude from Tertullian's opposition to baby baptism? Philip Schaff infers the following:

'The baptism of children was not yet at that time enjoined, but left to the option of Christian parents. Otherwise Tertullian would hardly have contested it with so much decision.' (*History of the Apostolic Church*, vol. 2, p. 271.)

Neander also considers Terullian's protest:

'a proof that the practice had not as yet come to be regarded as an apostolic institution; for otherwise he would hardly have ventured to express himself so strongly against it.' (*Church History*, vol. 1, p. 425.)

Thus we are confronted with the inescapable fact that as late as A.D. 200 baby baptism was regarded as optional. Obviously the Christians of the first two centuries did not consider baptism of babies to be either a divine ordinance or an apostolic institution. To conclude our survey of the first two centuries, we quote from the learned Dutch theologian, Venema (whose summary of the evidence will be found in Appendix B):

> 'Paedobaptism cannot be certainly proved to have been practised before the times of Tertullian ... These are the things that may be affirmed with apparent certainty, concerning the antiquity of baby baptism, after the times of the apostles; for more are maintained without solid foundation.'

In the light of these historical facts, acknowledged by Paedobaptist historians, we cannot but be astonished to find A.A. Hodge writing:

> 'The practice of infant baptism is an institution which exists as a fact, and prevails throughout the universal church, with the exception of the modern Baptists.'
> 'We find it noticed in *the very earliest records*, as *a universal custom*, and *an apostolic tradition*. This is acknowledged by Tertullian.' (*Outlines of Theology*, p. 504.)

The last quotation contains assertions, which Hodge italicises, every one of which is, in the words of Venema, 'without solid foundation.' To support his statement, Hodge writes:

> 'Origen born of Christian parents in Egypt, A.D. 185, declares that "the church had received the tradition from the apostles". St. Augustine, born A.D. 354, declares that this "doctrine is held by the whole church, not instituted by councils, but always retained."' (Op. cit. p. 505.)

Are the writings of Origen and Augustine 'the very earliest records?' Where does Tertullian teach that baby baptism was either a universal custom or an apostolic tradition? Had he thought it an apostolic tradition, he would not have opposed it.

J.C.Ryle is no more accurate when he writes:

> I might show that infant baptism was uniformly practised
> by all the early Christians. Every Christian writer of any
> repute during the first 1500 years after Christ, with the single
> gle exception perhaps of Tertullian, speaks of infant baptism
> as a custom which the church has always maintained.' (*Knots
> Untied*, p. 100.)

Are we to conclude that Ignatius and Clement of Rome are writers
of no repute? And what about the writings of Melito, Polycarp,
Theophilus of Antioch, Anthenagoras, Clement of Alexandria?
What about the epistle of Barnabas, the shepherd of Hermas, and the
Didache?

That men of such learning and piety as Hodge and Ryle should
make statements which are so easily demonstrated to be without
foundation, is astonishing to every student of church history.

If Tertullian was the first to make explicit reference to baby
baptism, it means that there is a silence on the subject of some 170
years from Pentecost. Now how are we to interpret this silence? It
is the custom of Protestants when disputing with Papists to say with
Bishop Burnet:

> 'The silence of the first and purest ages, about these things
> which are controverted among us, is evidence enough that
> they were not known to them; especially, since their
> Apologies which they wrote to the heathen for their religion
> and worship, wherein they give an abstract of their doctrines
> and a rubric of their worship, they never once mention these
> great evils for which we now accuse that (Roman) church.'
> (*Gibson's Preservative from Popery*, vol. 1, p. 272f.)

Again, Bingham employs this form of argument against the
religious use of images:

> 'Of images or pictures there is not a syllable, which is at least
> a good negative argument, that there was no such thing then
> in their churches.' (*Antiquities of the Christian Church*, vol.
> 1, b. 8. chap. 8 para. 6.)

In the same manner John Owen argues against episcopacy:

> 'No instance can be given or hath been, for the space of two hundred years, or until the end of the second century, of any one person who had the care of more churches than one committed unto him, or did take the charge of them on himself.' (*Enquiry into Original Nature of the Churches,* Preface p. 24.)

Why not argue in the same manner against the baptism of infants? The Roman Catholic Church seeks to escape the force of this argument from silence by saying with Bellarmine that things which are generally known and daily practised, are not accustomed to be written; to which the worthy Protestant, Dr. Clagett, replies thus:

> 'But if this will do, it is impossible these men should ever be convinced. For when we charge them with innovation in any matters of doctrine and practice, if they can show that those things are written in the ancients, we are certainly gone that way; for this proves that to be well known, and commonly practised in the primitive times, which we pretend was but of yesterday. But if we can show that they were not written, we get nothing by it at all; for it seems the reasons they were not written is because they were generally known and daily practised.' (*Preservative from Popery,* vol. 8, p. 285.)

Doddridge is sufficiently candid to admit that:

> 'It is indeed surprising that nothing more express is to be met with in antiquity upon this subject.' (*Miscellaneous Works*, p. 495.)

It certainly is on the supposition that baby baptism was the appointment of Christ, the practice of the apostles, and a constant custom in the Christian church. But Doddridge continues:

> 'But it is to be remembered that when infant baptism is first apparently mentioned, we read of no remonstrance against it as an innovation.'

But is not Tertullian the first author who apparently mentions baby baptism? And was he not against it? But supposing we had not read of the least remonstrance against baby baptism, when it was first mentioned, what then? Does it follow that it was practised from the beginning? Certainly not, for if this were the case, baby communion, the sign of the cross in baptism, trine immersion, consecration of the water of baptism, anointing with oil at baptism, the giving of milk and honey to the person baptized, etc. must be received as of divine appointment, because we read of no protest being made against them when first apparently mentioned.

And now to conclude. A survey of all the historical evidence of the first two centuries reveals that baptizing babies was introduced into the Christian church towards the end of the second century. In the words of the German historian, Dr. L. Lange:

> 'It must now be granted by every reader of holy Scripture and Christian antiquity, that the baptism of new-born children was altogether unknown to primitive Christianity. (*History of Protestantism*, p. 221.)

Chapter 10
Arguments from the Old Testament

So far it has been our principal concern to ascertain the historical facts regarding the practice of baby baptism. We have made a chronological review of baptism as administered by the Jews, by John, by Christ, by the apostles and first Christians, and by the church in the first two centuries. From the facts it was inferred that the baptism of babies is unauthorized by the New Testament, and it will be remembered that the logicality of this inference was admitted by B.B. Warfield when he wrote:

> 'The warrant for infant baptism is not to be sought in the New Testament but in the Old Testament.' (*Studies in Theology*, p. 399.)

It is time for us to turn to the Old Testament to see if we can find any ground for baby baptism therein. But before we begin a detailed investigation, we will make some general remarks.

The first thing to notice is that Paedobaptists appeal to the Old Testament for authority regarding what is essentially a New Testament ordinance. Does this not indicate the weakness of their cause? J.A. James, a Congregational Paedobaptist, when opposing the state establishment of religion writes:

> 'As to the argument which is founded upon the Constitution of the Jewish Theocracy, we consider it so irrelevant and inapplicable, that the very attempt to bring it forward in support of a Christian institute, betrays at once the weakness of their cause.' (*On Dissent,* p. 10.)

Another disestablishmentarian Paedobaptist, Ralph Wardlaw, writes:

'In my sermon on Religious Establishments I have charged those who would make the national church of Israel a model — even in the principle of it — for the imitation of Christians, with wilfully going back to the worldly and corrupt state of things, that has 'waxed old and vanished away;' with taking as their model that which he by whom it was instituted has set aside; with giving preference to the "beggarly elements" and choosing the introduction and carnal condition of the church, rather than the spiritual which it introduced; with thus inverting God's procedure, and building again the things which he has destroyed. I repeat the charge.' (*The Scripture Argument,* p. 25.)

Of course Wardlaw recognizes the essential continuity of the people of God in all ages, but he rightly distinguishes between the Jewish nation and the Christian church. The relevance of this distinction to the subject of baby baptism will soon be apparent.

Our second point we will put in the form of a request. We ask that the proof from the Old Testament be plain and direct. The argument must be so simple, the inferences so straightforward and obvious, that an unlearned Christian can follow them. Such a request for plainness is not unprecedented. It is well known Roman Catholics are given to justifying scores of their customs and ceremonies by appealing to the Old Testament. Protestants generally answer them by arguing in the manner of Dean Sherlock:

'I would not be thought wholly to reject a plain and evident consequence from scripture; but yet I will never admit of a mere consequence to prove an institution, which must be delivered in plain terms, as all laws ought to be; and where I have no other proof, but some scripture-consequences, I shall not think it equivalent to a scripture-proof. If the consequences be plain and obvious, and such as every man sees it, I shall not question it: but remote, and dubious, and dis-rupted consequences, if we have no better evidence to be sure are a very ill foundation for articles of faith. Let our Protestants then tell such disputants, that for the institution of sacraments, and for articles of faith, he expects plain positive proofs: that, as much as the Protestant faith is charged with uncertainty, we desire a little more certainty for our faith, than mere inferences from scripture, and those none of the plainest neither.' (*Gibson's Preservative from Popery* vol. 11, p. 152.)

Likewise Bishop Ryle argues against the sacramental regenerationists:

'I say unhesitatingly, to those who hold the view that there are two regenerations, they can bring forward no plain text in proof of it.' (*Knots Untied*, p. 117.)

The request for a plain proof in the case of baptizing babies is not unreasonable, because if God intended all Christians to have their children baptized, we may suppose that he would have left some plain directions for their guidance. As John Owen somewhere remarks:

'Every thing in scripture is so plain as that the meanest believer may understand all that belongs unto his duty or is necessary unto his happiness.'

The path of duty, like the way of holiness, is such that 'wayfaring men, though fools, shall not err therein' (Is. 35:8).

When it is remembered that Christians are supposed to have their children baptized at the beginning of their Christian lives, surely the proof must be plain. In another connection Albert Barnes makes an acute observation when commenting on the phrase 'the doctrine of baptisms' which is listed as one of the principles of the doctrine of Christ (Heb. 6:2).

'To understand the true doctrine concerning baptism was one of the first principles to be learned then, as it is now, as baptism is the rite by which we are initiated into the church. This was supposed to be so simple, that young converts could understand it as one of the elements of true religion, and the teaching on that subject now should be made so plain that the humblest disciple may comprehend it. If it was an element or first principle of religion, if it was presumed that anyone who entered the church could understand it, can it be believed that it was then so perplexing and embarrassing as it is often made now? Can it be so believed that a vast array of learning, and a knowledge of languages, and a careful inquiry into the custom of ancient times, was needful in order that a candidate for baptism should understand its nature.' (*Commentary on Heb.* 6:2.)

The same applies to the subjects of baptism. The ground for baptizing babies, the meaning of baptism when given to babies, should be so plain that the humblest disciple may comprehend it. But this is not the case, as the reader will find when he examines the arguments from the Old Testament. The inferences are so remote, dubious, and disputed that he will probably say with J.C. Ryle:

'A few plain texts of Scripture are needed; and these texts have yet to be found.' (*Knots Untied,* p. 116.)

The very diversity of the grounds on which men down the centuries have sought to establish baby baptism, indicates that the Scripture affords no plain proof. Cyprian justified the practice by the supposed universality of divine grace and the necessity of baptism to salvation. Augustine built baby baptism on the faith of the Church. The English Reformers looked to the faith of the sponsors. Beza, with many others, argued from the 'holiness' of babies. Others argue from the concept of convenant relationship or church membership. The various grounds on which baby baptism has been established, are listed by H. Bushnell as:

'natural innocence, inherited depravity, and federal holiness; because of the infant's own character, the parents' piety, and the church's faith; for the reason that the child is an heir of salvation already, and in order to make it such.'

Would there be so many different proofs of baby baptism, if any one of them had been plain and obvious? B.B. Warfield writes:

'Let us confess that we do not all argue alike or aright. But is not this a proof rather of the firm establishment in our hearts of the practice?' (*Studies in Theology*, p. 406.)

Indeed it is, and hence men are so slow to give the practice up.

But this is not all. If the baptism of babies is allowed, the next question to be answered is, Whose children are entitled to baptism? Charles Hodge replies:

> 'This is a very delicate, difficult, and important question. No answer which can be given to it can be expected to give general satisfaction.' (*Systematic Theology,* vol. 3, p. 558.)

Then follow twenty pages on the various answers given at different times by men within the Reformed tradition. These pages would make very entertaining reading, if they were not so tragic. Everyone should read them for himself. He will see godly men groping in the dark, stumbling this way and that, making covenants external, internal, half-way, etc., no one quite agreeing with his predecessors. Would there be such a confusion if baby baptism were from heaven? We think not.

The diversity and complexity, not to mention the prolixity, of the Reformed proofs of baby baptism, make an exhaustive consideration of them impossible in the small space at our disposal. So we shall concentrate on an able and popular statement of the two main proofs currently circulating in the Reformed churches. This method of treatment will necessitate a certain amount of overlapping, but repetition has its place in matters so complicated.

Should readers already be convinced that baby baptism is unscriptual and anti-scriptural, let them turn to chapter fourteen. Those who are still unpersuaded or unshaken, should read the following three chapters very slowly and carefully, and if need be, more than once. They require the full concentration of a fresh mind.

Chapter 11
The 'Church' argument of Charles Hodge

During the past few years* no less than five of Charles Hodge's books have been reprinted in Britain. amounting in all to some 3,642 pages. Being good value for money, they are deservedly gaining a wide circulation and exercising an increasing influence among Evangelicals, in view of which it is fitting and timely for us to examine Hodge's argument for baby baptism, as set out in his three volumed *Systematic Theology*.

Hodge begins the subject thus:

> 'The question, who are the proper subjects of baptism? is determined by the design of the ordinance and the practice of the apostles.' (Vol. 3, p. 540.)

Agreed. The design of the ordinance is clear from the command of Christ, as Hodge elsewhere admits:

> 'When Christ commanded the apostles to make disciples, baptizing them, etc., he obviously intended that baptism should be a badge of discipleship, or that by that rite his followers should acknowledge their relation to him.' (*The Way of Life*, p. 179.)

As for the practice of the apostles,

> 'In every case on record of their administering the rite, it was on condition of a profession of faith on the part of the recipient.' (Vol. 3, p. 541.)

And so both the command of Christ and the practice of the apostles lead to the same conclusion — that the proper subjects of baptism are those who profess faith in Christ and promise allegiance to him. Babies cannot profess faith or promise allegiance, therefore they are not the proper subjects of baptism. If then, as Hodge stipulates, the question, who are the proper subjects of baptism? is determined by the design of the ordinance and the practice of the apostles, the answer is simply, professing believers. To baptize those who do not profess faith — and this includes babies — is to go against both the design of baptism and the practice of the apostles.

Hodge, acknowledging this to be a real problem, writes:

'The difficulty on this subject is that baptism from its very nature involves a profession of faith: it is the way in which by the ordinance of Christ, he is to be confessed before men; but infants are incapable of making such a confession, therefore they are not the proper subjects of baptism.' (Vol. 3, p. 546.)

So it is that Hodge states the inference, feels its weight, calls it a difficulty and, as we shall see, leaves it unanswered. He goes on to state the problem in another form:

'The sacraments belong to the members of the church; but the church is the company of believers; infants cannot exercise faith, therefore they are not members of the church, and consequently ought not to be baptized.' (Vol. 3, p. 546f.)

Why he chooses to express the difficulty in this alternative form will soon be apparent.

'In order to justify the baptism of infants we must attain and authenticate such an idea of the church as that it shall i n - clude the children of believing parents.' (Vol. 3, p. 547.)

It will be noticed in order to justify the baptism of babies, Hodge turns from the design of baptism and the practice of the apostles to a certain idea of the church.

Hodge observes that 'the word Church is used in Scripture and in common life, in many different senses.' He lists five such meanings, the first of which is 'the whole body of the elect.' The remaining four have to do with *professed* believers. There is no mention of babies. Unlike so many theologians who build the baptizing of babies on their doctrine of the church. Hodge obliges us by giving a definition of the word church.

'In the present discussion, by the Church is meant what is called the visible Church; that is, the whole body of those who profess the true religion.' (Vol. 3, p. 547.)

Notice the word *profess*. Babies cannot profess, therefore this definition excludes babies from the visible church. This is scarcely a good beginning. The aim of his eight propositions is to 'attain and authenticate such an idea of the church as that it shall include the children of believing parents.' If Hodge is successful, he will prove his initial definition incorrect.

At this point a protest needs to be made against the lax use of the word Church by Paedobaptists, who flit from one meaning of the word to another, the effect of which is confusing, to say the least. As an instance of what we mean, take Bannerman in chapter one of his Church of Christ where he gives five meanings of the word Church, each of which he seeks to prove from Scripture. Then in chapter three he uses the word Church in a *sixth* sense, namely as consisting of 'all those who profess the faith of Christ, together with their children' (vol. 1, p. 29). This time he cites no scripture in support of this meaning. Now is this not misleading? Surely a word of so many diverse meanings ought not to be used in a sense for which there is no scriptural warrant, since this only adds to the confusion.

Returning to Hodge, we are glad that he has obliged us with his definition, though we are sorry that his very definition excludes babies from the outset. What Hodge says of the word sacrament, can be said of the word church:

'It is not from a word of such latitude of meaning that the nature or subjects of the Christian ordinances can be learned. (*The Way of Life*, p. 180.)

In order to ascertain his desired end Hodge lays down eight propositions:

'1. The Visible Church is a Divine Institution.' We will refer to this debatable proposition later.

'2. The Visible Church does not consist exclusively of the Regenerate.' Agreed. According to Hodge's definition, the visible church consists of 'the whole body of those who profess the true religion' i.e. true believers and mere professors. Babies are not included because they do not profess to believe, either sincerely or insincerely.

'3. The Commonwealth of Israel was the Church.' The first thing that strikes us about this proposition is that Hodge, in seeking to attain and authenticate a certain idea of the Christian church, turns to the Old Testament. This is very surprising because only four pages before Hodge states that the Romish theory of the church is 'derived from the ancient theocracy and from the analogy between the Church and a civil commonwealth' (p. 543). Did we not know Hodge to be a Protestant stalwart, we might think he was on the road to Rome!

Hodge's appeal to the Old Testament suggests that it is impossible to derive the desired idea of the Christian church from the New Testament.

That the Commonwealth of Israel cannot be equated with the church is clear from Hodge's definition of the word church: 'the whole body of those who profess the true religion.' As seen before, babies cannot profess, therefore cannot be members of the visible church. Hence the correct equation is

The commonwealth of Israel = the visible church + babies

Twenty years before Hodge published his Systematic Theology, he wrote in October, 1853 Princeton Review:

'It is to be remembered that there were two covenants made with Abraham. By the one, his natural descendants through Isaac were constituted a commonwealth — an external, visible community. By the other, his spiritual descendants were constituted a church. There cannot be a greater mistake than to confound the national covenant with the covenant of grace, and the commonwealth founded on the one with the church founded on the other. When Christ came, the commonwealth was abolished, and there was nothing put in its place. A church remained ... a spiritual society with spiritual promises, on the condition of faith in Christ.' (p. 684f.)

At first sight the Professor seems to contradict himself. But a closer study of his words reveals that in this paragraph, by church he means the invisible church, the sum total of those who possess true faith. Hence babies were in the commonwealth but not in the invisible church because they did not meet the conditions of faith in Christ.

And so we see that Jewish babies, while members of the commonwealth, were not members of the visible church because did not profess the true religion, nor were they members of the invisible church because they did not possess faith in the coming Saviour.

'4. The church under the New Dispensation is identical with that under the Old.' We agree with Hodge that 'our Saviour was the Saviour of the saints who lived before his advent in the flesh' (p. 551), and that 'the faith which saved Abraham was, both as to its nature and as to its object, that which is the condition of salvation under the gospel' (p. 551f.). But this is not to say that 'God has ever had but one church in the world' (p. 551). In this section Hodge forgets his definition of the word church. All that he writes on page 551 refers to the invisible church, not the visible church. There cannot be a greater mistake than to confuse the visible church with the invisible.

It is true that 'the (invisible) church under the new dispensation is identical with that under the old' in the sense that every member of each possesses faith in the same Saviour. It is also true that 'the (visible) church under the new dispensation is identical with that under the old' in the sense that every member of each professes faith in the same Saviour. And thus it is true that 'the church under the new dispensation is identical with that under the old' in the sense that, according to Hodge's own definition, babies are excluded from both.

'5. The terms of admission into the church before the Advent were the same that are required for admission into the Christian church.' Again it is necessary to watch this word church. First, consider the terms of admission into the visible church before the Advent, i.e. 'the whole body of those who professed the true religion' under the old dispensation. Those who were born Jews became members of the visible church when they personally professed the Jewish religion. Those who were born outside the Jewish commonwealth became members of the visible church upon professing the Jewish faith. What made them members was their profession. Whether Jew or Gentile, male or female, they became members of the Jewish visible church upon their profession of the Jewish faith.

Secondly, consider the terms of admission into the Jewish commonwealth. Those who were born Jews, both males and females, were members of the commonwealth by birth. In the case of proselytes from other nations, upon their profession of the Jewish religion, two things happened: (1) adults with their children became members of the commonwealth or state; (2) adults, in virtue of their profession, became members of the visible church.

By now it will be clear to everyone how inappropriate and confusing it is to apply the concept of a visible church to the Jews under the Old Testament.

Let it be said again that the terms of admission into the visible church under the new dispensation are to be directly deduced from the New Testament, not remotely inferred from the Old Testament. As was seen in previous chapters, only *professed* believers were recognized as members of the visible church (or churches) in New Testament times.

'6. Babies were members of the church under the Old Testament'. Hodge affirms that 'this is conclusively proved by the fact that babies by the command of God were circumcised on the eighth day after their birth.' (p. 552). But were the females circumcised? No. And so if the fact that males were circumcised conclusively proves they were members of the church, the fact that females were not circumcised proves that they were not members of the church. In short, the Jewish church was composed of males only!

In our discussion of proposition number 3, we saw that babies, because they neither profess nor possess faith in Christ, are neither members of the visible or invisible Church.

'7. There is nothing in the New Testament which justifies the exclusion of the children of believers from membership in the church.' Since Hodge has failed to prove that babies were members of the church (visible or invisible) in the Old Testament, this proposition should be altered to read: there is nothing in the Old

Testament which justifies the inclusion of the children of believers as members of the church.

Hodge speaks of children being deprived of their birthright when baptism is denied them. Some writers intimate that Antipaedobaptists, in withholding baptism from their offspring, do not love their children as they should. To which we reply that we refuse to let our natural love for them lead us to pervert the ordinance of Christian baptism. We do not baptize them, but we pray for them, we pray with them, we teach them the Scriptures from childhood, we take them to 'church' with us; in short, we do all that we think will profit their souls. If baptism conveys some grace or favour, some status or privilege, some blessing or benefit, please tell us what it is. Our reformed brethren do not believe in baptismal regeneration — and we unite with them in opposing all who do — but what does baptism do to babies? What is the precise difference between the children of believers who have been baptized and those who have not? If we are depriving our children of some great blessing, we would like to be informed what it is.

But the fact is that Evangelical Paedobaptists cannot tell us the profit of baptism when administered to babies, as William Cunningham admits:

'There is a great difficulty — a difficulty which Scripture does not afford us adequate material for removing — in laying down any distinct and definite doctrine as to the bearing and efficacy of baptism in the case of babies.' (*The Reformers and the Theology of the Reformation,* p. 246.)

In other words, if we ask Cunningham, What profit is there in baptizing babies? he replies, I cannot say; the Scripture is silent! We admire his candour, but wonder how he can continue to use this means of mysterious grace!

If the Scripture is silent to Cunningham, it speaks most audibly to Hodge, for he writes:

'Those parents sin grievously against the souls of their children who neglect to consecrate them to God in the ordinance of baptism. Do let the little ones have their names written in the Lamb's book of life, even if they afterwards choose to erase them. Being thus enrolled may be the means of their salvation.' (Vol. 3, p. 588.)

This is astounding. Is Hodge serious? Does he really believe that the Lamb's book of life is, as it were, a heavenly baptismal roll?

Hodge seems to imply that those children who die before choosing to erase their names from the Lamb's book of life, will of course be saved. It logically follows that those who die in infancy unbaptized, perish because their names are not written in the Lamb's book of life. But Hodge does not believe this, for elsewhere he teaches that:

'All who die in infancy are saved.' (Vol. 1, p. 26.)

This means, we take it, that all who die in infancy have their names written in the Lamb's book of life. Now since the majority of those dying in infancy are unbaptized, baptism cannot write their names in the Lamb's book of life. Again we ask. What profit is there in baby baptism?

'8. Children need, and are capable of receiving the benefits of redemption.' This we will not dispute, but if it follows that children are therefore to be baptized, it also follows that all who have not sinned against the Holy Spirit ought to be baptized because all such need, and are capable of receiving, the benefits of redemption. If this argument justifies the baptism of some babies, it justifies the baptism of *all* babies. Indeed it warrants the indiscriminate baptism of adults. This argument, then, proves too much, and in the words of another able advocate of Paedobaptism, Peter Edwards:

'It is a rule in reasoning that that argument which proves too much destroys itself.' (*Candid Reasons*, p. 152).

By means of the above eight propositions Hodge seeks to attain and authenticate such an idea of the church as that shall include the children of believing parents, with what success the reader must judge.

* Written in 1962 — Editor

Chapter 12
The 'Covenant' Argument of
J. G. Vos

A recent and representative statement of another Reformed proof of baby baptism is to be found in the 1959 January-March issue of *Blue Banner Faith and Life** in an article written by the editor, Dr. J. G. Vos, who has kindly consented to quotations being taken therefrom. We shall quote him at length in order that he might be allowed to speak for himself.

Dr. Vos begins:

> 'Infant baptism is a Scriptural practice which does not depend upon isolated proof-texts' (presumably because there aren't any!). 'It follows logically from other truths of the Scriptures; the proof may be stated, essentially, in the following form:
>
> (a) Baptism is a sign and seal of the Covenant of Grace.
> (b) The children of believers are included in the Covenant of Grace.
> (c) Therefore the children of believers are entitled to baptism which is a sign and seal of the Covenant of Grace.' (p. 37.)

*This is a quarterly publication devoted to expounding, defending and applying the system of doctrine set forth in the Word of God and summarized in the standards of the Reformed Presbyterian (Covenanter) Church. Copies of this excellent magazine may be obtained from Dr. J. G. Vos, 3408 7th Avenue, Beaver Falls, Pennsylvania, U.S.A.

The illogicality of this argument is easily demonstrated. In proposition (a) replace 'baptisj' by 'the Lord's Supper', which, according to reformed teaching, is also a sign and seal of the Covenant of Grace. Inference (c) now reads: Therefore the children of believers are entitled to the Lord's Supper. In other words, this very argument justifies the practice of baby communion. But this Dr. Vos will not allow. So again it is a case of 'that argument which proves too much destroys itself.'

Let us examine propositions (a) and (b) and inference (c).

(a) Baptism is a sign and seal of the Covenant of Grace. Like the word Church, the term Covenant of Grace is capable of more than one meaning, and consequently requires precise definition. For, as Bishop Ryle remarks, 'the absence of accurate definition is the very life of religious controversy.'

Dr. Vos defines the Covenant of Grace as follows:

> 'Back in eternity God the Father entered into the Covenant of Grace with his only begotten Son, Jesus Christ, the sec-ond Adam, as the representative of all the people whom God had elected to eternal life. John 17:2' (p. 27.)

Two things are to be noted: the Covenant of Grace was made with the Son; the parties interested or concerned in the Covenant of Grace are the elect.

Baptism as a sign

What is meant by calling baptism a sign of the Covenant of Grace? There are two possible answers. First, baptism is a sign that God has made a covenant with his Son to save all the elect. Accordingly, baptism is the sign of an objective promise, and has no reference at all to the character and condition of the person baptized. If an objective promise is all that baptism signifies, it would seem very desirable to baptize indiscriminately with a view to proclaiming to all, that God has promised to save all the elect, i.e. all who believe in his Son.

The other meaning is that baptism is a sign that the person baptized is one of those in the Covenant of Grace, i.e. one of the elect unto salvation. This is to say that baptism is the sign of a subjective state. In this case, it follows that the sign is to be given to those who give reasonable evidence of having the thing signified, i.e. to those who give evidence of being elect. As William Cunningham writes:

> 'Signifying and sealing naturally suggests the idea, that the things signified and sealed not only exist, but are actually possessed by those to whom they are signified and sealed.' (*The Reformers and the Theology of the Reformation*, p. 278.)

Hence, it must be shown from Scripture that the children of believers are in the Covenant of Grace, i.e. elect unto salvation, before baptism can be administered properly to them — assuming that baptism is a sign of the Covenant of Grace, which assertion requires proof.

Whether or not baptism is a sign of the Covenant of Grace, objectively or subjectively, it cannot be denied that baptism, in the words of Calvin, is 'partly an outward sign of faith'. But this is not the case when baptism is administered to babies, even to elect babies. In short, baptism loses part of its significance even if it is administered to babies as a sign of the Covenant of Grace.

Baptism as a seal

What is meant by calling baptism a seal of the Covenant of Grace? This likewise has two possible answers. First, baptism is a seal of the promise that God made with his Son to save all the elect. According to this view, baptism is a seal in general but not in particular; it vouches for God's promise of grace at large, but does not attest the personal salvation of the party baptized.

The other view is that baptism pledges, or guarantees that the person baptized is in the Covenant of Grace, i.e. is elect. This latter meaning obviously needs qualification which Dr. Vos quickly makes:

> 'Where baptism is rightly used, with faith in Christ, it serves as a 'seal' or divinely-given certificate of the benefits of Christ's redemption.' (p. 38.)

Thus, baptism is not a seal where there is no faith in Christ. Hence baptism is not a seal to a person baptized as a baby, but becomes so when the person believes. This means that baptism is not a seal in and of itself.

The fact that Dr. Vos has to make his qualification 'with faith in Christ' shows that baptism is not really a seal at all. To illustrate our point, in Revelation 7:3 we read of 144,000 servants of God sealed in their foreheads. The seal was a mark by which they were distinguished from others (Revelation 9:4). Now does baptism infallibly distinguish Christians from others? Certainly not.

Therefore baptism is not a seal. If it be asked, 'What is the seal of the Covenant of Grace?' the answer is found by asking 'What is it that distinguishes Christians from others?' And what is that? The Holy Spirit (Romans 8:9) and hence the Holy Spirit is called a seal (Ephesians 1:13; 4:30 compare John 6:27). It is not water but the Spirit which is the seal of the Covenant of Grace. If baptism were a seal of the Covenant of Grace in the subjective sense, then all who were baptized would be marked out as servants of God and would consequently be saved.

But, it will be said, is not circumcision called a seal in Romans 4:11? Indeed it is, but what did circumcision seal? Did it seal or guarantee that everyone circumcised was in the Covenant of Grace, i.e. elect unto salvation? Not at all, as the history of the Jews too clearly shows. Circumcision is called 'a seal of the righteousness of the faith' of Abraham, on which Professor John Murray comments:

'The seal is that which God himself appended to assure Abraham that the faith he exercised to God's promise was accepted by God.' (*The Epistle to the Romans,* vol. 1, p. 138.)

Circumcision was a seal to Abraham, it assured Abraham; it was not a seal to Abraham's posterity in the sense that it assured them that they personally had the righteousness of faith. Circumcision did not guarantee the person circumcised that he was justified in the sight of God, though many of the Jews mistakenly believed this. And so we cannot agree with Dr. Vos that 'circumcision was a sign and seal of partaking of the benefits of the Covenant of Grace, under the Old Testament' (p. 38). However, we are willing to call circumcision a seal of the righteousness of faith, in the sense that circumcision guaranteed to all — women as well as men, Gentiles as well as Jews

— that God justifies those who believe his promises.

To call the covenant of circumcision (Acts 7:8) the Covenant of Grace is to confound and confuse things that differ. To be sure, the covenant of circumcision was a covenant of grace, and was made as a result of the covenant of grace (or covenant of redemption as others call it). The differences between the covenant of grace and the covenant of circumcision are as follows:

(1) the covenant of grace was made with Christ, whereas the covenant of circumcision was made with Abraham;

(2) the covenant of grace promised spiritual blessings to all believers, whereas the covenant of circumcision, whilst promising the blessing of justification by faith in the seed of Abraham, also promised certain material blessings to those descended from Abraham after the flesh, which blessings are not promised to all persons in the Covenant of Grace.

It is to be regretted that the practice of calling baptism a seal still continues, notwithstanding the confusion it has occasioned among great theologians and the delusion it has brought to multitudes of simple believers. The reason the practice continues is suggested by William Cunningham:

'The sacraments are not seals of spiritual blessings in any such sense as implies, that they are attestations to the personal character or spiritual condition of those who receive them, or, that the mere reception of the sacraments is to be held as of itself furnishing a proof, or even a presumption, that those receiving them are true believers, and may be assured that they have reached a condition of safety. This is a point about which much ignorance and confusion prevail, and which it may be proper to explain somewhat fully.

It is the almost universal practice of divines to apply the word "seal" to the sacraments, and to call them "sealing ordinances". But what they usually mean by the application of this term to the sacraments, it is not easy to determine. Indeed, we can scarcely resist the impression, that many divines, in professing to explain the function or influence of the sacraments as seals, have recourse to what is a little better than an intentional ambiguity of language, as if they were anxious to insinuate, that there is something very important

and mysterious in this sealing, while yet they carefully avoid
giving any clear and definite explanation of what it means, as
if from a lurking apprehension that the attempt to do so would
make the whole mystery "evaporate in their hands." (*British
and Foreign Evangelical Review*, 1860, p. 932.)

Let us now examine Dr. Vos' second proposition.

(b) The children of believers are included in the Covenant of
Grace.

This statement deserves the closest attention because, in the
words of Dr. Vos,

> 'The real proof of infant baptism depends on the truth that the
> children of believers are included in the Covenant of Grace.'
> (p. 37.)

In support of his proposition he quotes Genesis 17:7-10; Acts 2:39;
Malachi 2:15; 1 Corinthians 7:14. Now it will be seen that if these
verses imply that some of the children of believers are in the
Covenant of Grace, they imply that all are, without exception. In
others words, all the children of believers are elect and will be saved.
But this is contrary to experience, as Dr. Vos acknowledges:

> 'It must be admitted that the fact that the children of believers
> are included in the Covenant of Grace does not imply that
> all children of believers, without exception, are elect per-
> sons who shall receive eternal life.' (p. 36.)

Thus, experience contradicts the supposed implications of the
verses quoted. Furthermore, if the fact that children of believers are
included in the Covenant of Grace does not imply that all children
of believers are elect persons, it does not imply that any of them are.

Dr. Vos continues:

> 'All are born in the covenant but some turn out to be
> covenant-breakers and are eternally lost.'

In other words, the Covenant of Grace is breakable. To us this
sounds more like a Covenant of Works.

Dr. Vos is aware of this difficulty and proposes a further

refinement or adjustment:

> 'There are two phases of the Covenant of Grace, (a) a legal
> or external phase, and (b) a vital or spiritual phase. We may
> think of these two phases as two circles, one within the other
> — an outer and an inner circle. Every child born of believing
> parents is in the outer circle, the legal or external sphere of
> the Covenant of Grace. But only those truly born again are in
> the inner circle, the vital or spiritual sphere of the Covenant
> of Grace. Some people born in the external sphere, the outer
> circle, are non-elect persons and never come to Christ. Every
> one that is of the elect will, at some time in his life, come into
> the inner circle, the vital or spiritual sphere.' (p. 36.)

Outer circle! Inner circle! Vital sphere! External sphere! We are
beginning to get dizzy! We are not sure if we are in two dimensions
or three! If we find this so hard to follow, we pity the new convert
from paganism.

The next thing for us to understand is, What is meant by saying
that the children of believers are included in the Covenant of Grace?
Dr. Vos thus:

> 'It means:
> (a) that all children of believers are born in the external sphere
> of the Covenant of Grace
> (b) that the covenant privileges belong to them by birth
> (c) that the covenant obligations rest upon them from infancy
> (d) that it must be assumed that they are elect and regenerate
> in the absence of evidence which would lead to the contrary
> conclusion.' (p. 38.)

As to (a) these words do not provide much light, for what is this
external sphere? The concept of the external sphere of the Covenant
of Grace is practically the same as that of sacramental regeneration,
concerning which Bishop Ryle writes:

> 'A regeneration which only means admission into a state of
> ecclesiastical privilege may be ancient and primitive for
> anything I know. But something more than this is needed. A
> few plain texts of Scripture are needed; and these have yet

to be found. Such a notion of regeneration ... renders it necessary to invent the awkward theory that there are two regenerations, and is thus eminently calculated to confuse the minds of unlearned people, and introduce false doctrine.' (*Knots Untied,* p. 116.)

The corresponding theory that there are two spheres of the Covenant of Grace is equally unscriptual, awkward, and calculated to confuse.

As to (b), what are these covenant privileges? Obviously the children of Christians have many advantages over children born in a non-Christian home. These advantages could be called privileges, but not in the sense that they are the special and exclusive possession of the children of believers. Children with Christian foster parents (though the children of unbelievers), children in Christian orphanages, and even children from pagan homes who attend Sunday School, and Weeknight Youth Meetings (assuming these are spiritual), share these privileges to some extent.

As to (c), what are these covenant obligations? Are they not repentance and faith? And are they not binding on all who hear the gospel, not just the children of the covenant?

As to (d), what ground have we for assuming our children are elect? Which Scripture supports such an assumption? The texts quoted above prove, according to Dr. Vos' interpretation, that all the children of believers are in the Covenant of Grace. If these texts mean, as Dr. Vos thinks, that all children of believers are in the external sphere of the covenant, which texts promise that all, or indeed any, of them will necessarily pass into the inner sphere? There are cases — it is true, they are exceptional — where none of the children come into the inner sphere. What of the covenant in these cases?

Besides assuming them to be elect, Dr. Vos tells us to assume they are regenerate. Can someone be regenerate and not show it? Not according to Professor John Murray. (See *Redemption Accomplished and Applied,* p. 103f. or 127f.) Not according to J. C Ryle:

'Many divines maintain that we may call people 'regener-ate' in whom none of the marks just described are seen, or even were seen since they were born. They tell us, in short, that people may possess the gift of the Spirit, and the grace of Regeneration when neither the gift nor the grace can be seen.

Such a doctrine appears to me dangerous in the highest degree.' (*Knots Untied*, p. 132.)

It certainly is, as every pastor of souls knows. Too many parents
presume their children are Christians, treat them as such, and find to
their horror, perhaps when they leave home, that they are anything
but Christians. It is much safer for parents to assume they are
children of the flesh (which they are!) until they are born of the
Spirit. Let us account them regenerate when we see them converted.
In the words of William Cunningham:

> 'Nothing should ever be regarded as furnishing evidence of
> regeneration, except the appropriate proofs of an actual
> renovation of the moral nature, exhibited in each case i n -
> dividually; and that, until these proofs appear, every one,
> whether baptized or not, should be treated and dealt with in
> all respects as if he were unregenerate, and still needed to be
> born again of the word of God through the belief of the truth.'
> (*The Reformers and the Theology of the Reformation*, p. 291.)

To return to (b). As far as we can understand, the great covenant
privilege supposed to belong to children of believers is that if they
die in infancy or before coming to the years of discretion, they are
certainly saved. Dr. Vos writes:

> 'We should not entertain the slightest doubt that all covenant
> children which die before reaching years of discretion are of
> the elect and are saved by the mysterious operation of the
> Holy Spirit.' (p. 43.)

His argument to support this is as follows:

> 'God's covenant established with Abraham (Genesis 17:1-
> 14) proves that every child of believing parents is born within
> the Covenant of Grace. It is true that some of the children of
> believing parents are not of the elect, and turn out to the
> covenant-breakers. But a baby that dies before r e a c h i n g
> the years of discretion cannot be a covenant-breaker; it
> cannot despise and violate the obligation of the Covenant
> of Grace. Therefore we have the best reasons for believing
> that all children of believing parents dying in infancy are not

only in the Covenant of Grace, but also of the number of the elect and shall certainly be saved.' (p. 43.)

It seems that all this talk about covenant privileges culminates in this comfort, a comfort the bereaved Christian parents long to have, a comfort which their pastor longs to give. But Dr. Vos' comforting words are not derived from his doctrine of the covenant. Experience teaches us that if our children attain the age of accountability, it is possible that one or more of them may not believe unto salvation. Consequently it is natural to wonder if one or more of those children dying in infancy are elect or not. There is nothing in the covenant doctrine to dispel this doubt.

And what of non-covenant children dying in infancy? Are they saved? Most Reformed theologians think so. If so how? Do they pass into the inner sphere without going through the outer sphere? Concerning the salvation of babies we are inclined to say concerning all babies what Dr. Vos confines to non-covenant children:

'Since the Bible says nothing on this subject, nothing can be proved concerning it, one way or the other. We must respect the silences of Scripture. This is a question that may safely be left to the justice and mercy of God.' (p. 43.)

We now turn to consider Dr. Vos' inference (c) from the propositions (a) and (b).

(c) Therefore the children of believers are entitled to baptism, which is a sign and seal of the Covenant of Grace. We have already noticed that Dr. Vos denies the parallel inference namely, that the children of believers are entitled to the Lord's Supper.

If for argument's sake we grant propositions (a) and (b) we will now show that inference (c) does not necessarily follow. Let us consider an example in the Old Testament. It will not be denied that the Jewish females had as great a part and interest in the covenant made with Abraham as had the males. Here then we have a case of persons in covenant who are yet without the sign of the covenant, circumcision. To answer an obvious objection, it should be remembered that a certain kind of circumcision was given to females by the Egyptians, and a similar practice could easily have prevailed among the Jews. Now the reason the Jewish males were circumcised was not that they were in covenant with God — the females were equally so — but because God ordered the males to be circumcised. Had it so pleased him, he need never have given any sign at all, in which case both males and females would have been in covenant with him without having any sign to that effect.

Thus, people may be in covenant who are without the sign of the covenant, and the sole reason for giving all or some the sign of the covenant is the commandment of God. It follows that even if the children of believers were in some special covenant relationship, this of itself does not entitle them to the sign of that covenant. The sign is to be given only as the Lord commands — perhaps to the males only, perhaps to the females, perhaps to both, perhaps to neither. In previous chapters we have seen that the Lord has not commanded that babies should be baptized, whether male or female, so that Christians are no more required to baptize their babies than the Jews are required to circumcise their females.

In conclusion, the words of J. C. Ryle concerning the idea of two regenerations are very applicable to the theory of two phases of the Covenant of Grace;

> 'I say unhesitatingly, that those who hold the view that there are two regenerations, can bring forward no plain text in proof of it. I firmly believe that no plain reader of the Bible only would ever find this view there for himself; and that goes very far to make me suspect it is an idea of man's invention.' (*Knots Untied*, p. 117.)

Chapter 13
Baptism of Babies is Retrogression

Not all Paedobaptists agree with Hodge and Vos that baptism is to be confined to those babies born within the church or covenant. The godly Archbishop Leighton argues against the strict Reformed view thus:

> 'Touching baptism, freely my thought is, it is a weak n o -tion taken on trust almost generally, to consider so much, or at all, the qualifications of parents. Either it is a benefit to babies, or it is not. If none, why then administer it at all? But if it be, then why should the poor innocents be prejudged for the parents' cause, if he professes but so much of a Christian, as to offer his child to that ordinance? For that the parents' faith gives the child a right to it, is neither from Scripture nor any sound reason.' (*Select Works*, p. 518.)

How do the Reformed theologians answer that?

The Reformed theory of limiting baptism to the children of believers suffers from another defect. The baby's right to baptism is made to depend ultimately upon the baby's *physical* relationship to his parents. Matthew Henry writes:

> 'Infant baptism speaks an hereditary relation to God, that comes to us by descent.' (*Treatise on Baptism*, p. 193.)

Notice that it is 'hereditary' and 'comes by descent'. Does this not remind us of the Pharisees who thought their descent from Abraham entitled them to John's baptism? (See chapter 2).

It is true that in the Old Testament, God, in dispensing certain blessings and privileges, had respect unto birth and blood. What constituted a person a Jew was not his faith in Abraham's God but his physical descent from Abraham. Likewise what qualified a man for the priesthood was not his suitability for that office but the blood in his veins. All this is altered in the new dispensation in which the favours bestowed are pre-eminently spiritual and which, moreover, are given according to the grace of God who is no respecter of natural relationships. In the words of Patrick Fairburn,

> 'Undoubtedly the New Testament form (of the external ordinance of the Covenant of Grace) less distinctly recognizes the connection between parent and child — we should rather say, does not of itself recognize the connection at all; so much ought to be frankly conceded to those who disapprove of the practice of infant baptism, and will be conceded by all whose object is to ascertain truth rather than contend for an opinion.' (*Typology of Scripture,* vol. 1, p. 313f.)

This fact is given repeated emphasis in the New Testament, especially in the Gospel of John. In chapter 1 verse 13 John informs us that the right or privilege of being sons of God belongs to those born 'not of blood, nor of the will of the flesh, nor of the will of man, but of God'. William Hendriksen comments:

> 'The Jew was very slow to learn that in the new dispensation there are no special privileges based upon physical relationships.' (*The Gospel of John*, vol. 1, p. 81.)

Evidently the Jews are not the only ones who have been slow to learn this distinguishing feature of the new covenant. To baptize children on the ground of their physical relationship to their parents savours of Judaism. Baptizing babies involves a return to the kindergarten stage of the people of God. In short, baby baptism is retrogression. But this is not all. The confining of baptism to believers' children saviours of paganism. Albert Barnes, who in glowing terms can speak of the benefits of baby baptism and privileges belonging to the babies of believers, on Galatians 3:26-28 comments:

'In regard to this doctrine of Christianity, that there is neither "bond nor free" among those who are saved, or that they
are on a level in regard to salvation we may remark further,
that it is peculiar to Christianity. All other systems of religion
and philosophy make different ranks, and endeavour to pro-
mote a distinction or caste among men. They teach that
certain men are the favourites of heaven on account of their
birth or rank in life, or that they have peculiar facilities for
salvation. Thus, in India, the Brahmin is regarded as by his
birth a favourite of heaven, and all others are supposed to
be of a degraded rank. The great effort of men in their systems
of religion and philosophy has been to shew that there are
favoured ranks and classes, and to make permanent
distinctions on account of birth and blood.' (*Commentary* in
loc.)

Is not therefore the Reformed practice of baby baptism heathenish?
Is there not 'distinction on account of birth and blood' in the
advocacy of baptism for the children that have a believing parent?
Is not the great foundation, the grand and ever-recurring argument
for baby baptism, 'the connection of children with their parents?'
Reformed Paedobaptists, having put the children of believers in a
special class of their own, treat them quite differently from the
children of unbelievers. For example, Pierre Marcel writes
concerning the children of believers:

'For them the content of our message is not the same as that
which we address to proselytes.' (*The Biblical Doctrine of
Infant Baptism,* p. 135.)

The special class requires a special gospel! In what respects the
gospel is different when addressed to believers children Marcel does
not say. He goes on:

'Since they are within the covenant, the promises which
concern them, the demands of God, the possibility of their
responding to them, and also their responsibility, are quite
different.'

This statement is worthy of close examination.

First, 'the promises which concern them'. On page 109 Marcel depicts God as saying to believing parents: 'I will be your God and the God of your posterity after you. You will be saved together with your family.' Now if this is an unconditional promise, of course a different gospel must needs be preached to covenant children. It will not be 'Believe and be saved', but 'Believe that you are saved.' However, Marcel does not leave this promise without qualification:

> 'God in his grace undertakes with an oath to receive the children of believers as long as they live, on condition that these children in turn appropriate the promises by faith. If they ask him to be their Father, he will be.' (Op. cit. p. 109.)

True enough, but the very same thing may be said of all children, indeed of all the unconverted. If they ask God to be their Father, he will be. Marcel seems to imply that God has a greater desire for the salvation of believers' children that for those born and living outside the covenant. Even if this were granted, it would still have to be admitted that in many cases, this desire on God's part proves ineffectual. Perhaps Marcel implies that God has no desire for the salvation of those 'outside the covenant' — a tenet of High Calvinism, so obviously contrary to Scripture. Once let it be granted that God desires the salvation of all men (a desire which is nevertheless ineffectual in the case of the non-elect), let it be granted that God promises to be a Father to all who will take him as their God, and this special promise of the covenant to believers' children is seen to be nothing more than the general invitation of the gospel made to all men.

Secondly, 'the demands of God'. Marcel speaks of those in the covenant who have attained the age of accountability as 'under obligation to repent and believe' (p. 131). True enough, but the same obligation rests upon all who hear the gospel. The duty of the unregenerate 'in the covenant' is no different from the duty of the unregenerate 'out of the covenant'.

Thirdly, 'the possibility of their responding to them'. Marcel supposes the children of believers to be given grace which, if we understand him aright, is the basis of their responsibility to repent and believe. He writes:

'The grace of the covenant, in fact, is not always saving grace, absolutely efficacious and infallibly conducive to salvation; it is resistible grace which may suffer revolt and which involves the full responsibility of him who rejects it.' (p. 111.)

Resistible grace is supposed to make the recipient able (or more able?) to respond. Is Marcel making the measure of grace the measure of responsibility? This is a tenet of Arminianism. Besides, is it not true that resistible grace is given to all who hear the gospel? In fact, is not the gospel message itself the resistible grace of God? See 2 Corinthians 5:1. The possibility of believers' children responding to the gospel is no different from that of any others who may hear the gospel. One other point. Notice that the grace of the covenant is sometimes resistible. What comfort is it to Christian parents to know that their children have received resistible grace? Fourthly, 'their responsibility'. Marcel writes:

'The fact of being in the covenant with all the promises and benefits, lays an increased responsibility upon them. 'If I had not come,' says Christ, 'and spoken to them, they would not have had sin; but now they have no excuse for their sin.' (John 15:22.)' (p. 131.)

Agreed, but the same may be said of those outside the covenant who have persistently rejected the gospel.

In short, the children of believers are not really in a special class or category at all, and hence they need the same gospel as all children of wrath. William Hendriksen is right after all in stating that 'in the new dispensation there are no special privileges based upon physical relationships.'

Perhaps at this point someone will object that the children of Christians are not so privileged as the children of Jews under the old dispensation. If the Jews' children were given circumcision as the sign of the covenant, would we not expect baptism to be given to Christians' children? The reply to this objection is simple. Compare the privileges of God's ministerial servants in the Old and New Testaments. In the Old Testament the son of a priest, upon coming of age, was set apart for the priesthood. This was his by right of birth, and was conferred upon him without any regard to his moral character or suitability for that office. But in the New Testament the son of a gospel minister has no such automatic title to the gospel ministry. Are the children of Christian ministers, then, worse off than the children of Jewish priests? The comparison is odious.

Roman Catholics have used this same argument of comparison to good effect. They argue that if the places of worship in the Old Testament were elaborate and ornate, surely the places of worship under the new covenant should not be less beautified. Those who justify baby baptism by this argument of comparison will, if they consistently follow the principle in other cases, have to accept not only ornate churches, but priests, vestments, incense, etc. because all these had a part in the worship of God in the Old Testament, and it cannot be expected that God is worthy of less now!

The children of Jews and the children of Christians are equal in this respect — they must be saved by faith, not by receiving the sign of the covenant. As for those dying in infancy, BC or AD, born of Jews or Gentiles, Christians or non-Christians, the Scripture is, to our mind, silent.

Under the new covenant children are brought up in the full blaze of gospel light, whereas under the old covenant children enjoyed but a dim twilight of types and carnal ordinances. Who is it then who does not see that the children of Christians are much more privileged, in respect of knowledge, than the children of Jews? Our children may not receive the sign of the covenant, but this is no loss because just as 'circumcision profiteth, if thou keep the law' (Romans 2:25), so baptism profits, if you believe the gospel. Apart from fulfilling the condition of the covenant — works under the law, faith under the gospel — the sign of the covenant is utterly worthless. So that all that the children of Christians have lost is something of no saving value.

Chapter 14
The Evils of the Baptism of Babies

If baby baptism is unauthorized by, and inconsistent with, Holy Scripture, its continued practice in the churches of Christendom must be an evil, the magnitude of which we will now try to assess. First of all, baby baptism betrays the Reformed cause. As so many Lutheran scholars have admitted, baptism of babies cannot be established on the authority of Scripture alone. The result is that baptizing babies gives Roman Catholics a handle which many of their abler controversialists have used to good effect. For example, Bishop Bossuet writes:

> 'As touching infants, the pretended reformed say that their baptism is grounded on the authority of Scripture, but they bring us no place out of it, expressly affirming it, and what consequences they draw of the same, they are very far-fetched, not to say very doubtful, and too deceitful.' (*On the Holy Supper*, p. 127.)

Bossuet can afford to argue thus, because his church acknowledges the authority of tradition.

It is impossible to measure the harm done to the Protestant cause through the retention of paedobaptism. The Reformed churches profess to be governed solely by Scripture, but so long as they continue baptizing babies, so long will they be taunted by Roman Catholics (and others) for their manifest inconsistency.

Secondly, baby baptism necessitates an alteration in the meaning of Christian baptism. Additions to the Word of God invariably lead to alterations. It is a characteristic of human tradition always to make void some part or other of the commandments of God. Let John Brown of Edinburgh give some examples:

> 'Whenever human authority has found its way into the church of God, it has not rested satisfied with merely adding to the laws and institutions of Christ; it has always in some measure altered and annulled them. When, in the Roman Catholic church, so many ceremonies were added to the simple rite of the Lord's Supper, the result was that the one half of the original ordinance was abolished, the cup being denied to the laity. Wherever saints' days are observed on human authority, the Lord's Day, appointed by Divine authority, is neglected. Whenever the ministers of religion are supported by State endowments, the Divine financial law, "Let him who is taught in the word communicate unto him that teacheth in all good things" is superseded, and, as far as man can do it, repealed. When men introduce their own terms of communion, Christ's terms of communion are sure to be disregarded; and when, in the Presbyterian churches of this country, a host of unauthorized, or at any rate unappointed, services, were connected with an administration of the Lord's Supper; then an ordinance, which in the primitive age was observed every Lord's Day, was converted into an annual religious festival.
>
> The Christian church is even yet very imperfectly freed from the unholy influence and the mischievous operation of human authority. The house requires to be more carefully swept than it was at the reformation from popery, and a more thorough search must be made for the old leaven, that it may be completely cast out.' (*Discourses and Sayings of Our Lord,* vol. 1, p. 499.)

In chapter seven it was seen that the New Testament teaching as to the meaning and import of Christian baptism simply cannot apply to babies. Neither can the generally accepted descriptions of baptism. When baptism is administered to babies, it ceases to be

'a badge of discipleship' (Hodge, see p. 70)
'an outward sign of faith' (Calvin, see p. 27)

'a sign of regeneration or the new birth' (*Article of the Church of England.*)
'a sign and seal to the party baptized of his engrafting into Christ, of his remission of sins, and of his giving up unto God through Jesus Christ, to walk in newness of life.'
(*Westminster Confession*, 23. 1.)

The fact that it is necessary to alter the New Testament teaching respecting baptism in the case of babies, is in itself evidence that baptism is an addition.

If baby baptism were abolished and believer's baptism restored, men would have little difficulty in understanding the meaning of Christian baptism, as William Cunningham admits:

'If we were in the habit of witnessing adult baptism and if we formed our primary and full conceptions of the import a n d effects of the ordinance from the baptism of adults, the one sacrament would be as easily understood, and as definitely comprehended, as the other.' (*Historical Theology*, vol. 2, p. 145.)

Thus baby baptism complicates what is essentially a simple ordinance, and with what results we shall see in a moment.

Thirdly, baptizing babies destroys the appointed way of professing faith in Christ. Charles Hodge says of baptism that 'it is the way in which by the ordinance of Christ, he is to be confessed before men.' (*Systematic Theology*, vol.3, p., 546.) Experience teaches us that it is necessary to have some way of confessing Christ before men, some badge of discipleship. The appointed badge is baptism. Now those who baptize babies do not re-baptize upon profession of faith, and thus the unscriptural practice of baby baptism nullifies the Scriptural practice of believers' baptism.

Of course, it is theoretically possible to believe in two baptisms — an Ecclesiastical baptism to be given to people in infancy, and a Christian baptism to be given on profession of faith. Such Paedobaptists could well be called Anabaptists! They would at least be acquitted of the charge of nullifying the divine ordinance of believers' baptism. But, for obvious reasons, Paedobaptists are unwilling to take up such a theory, so that they cannot avoid the charge of perverting one of Christ's sacraments.

As just mentioned, experience teaches us that it is necessary to have some way of confessing Christ before men. If the way is not baptism, it must be something else, and Paeobaptists have been compelled by experience to introduce further additions to offset the subtraction of believers' baptism. And so we find them resorting to such ceremonies as Confirmation and such concepts as communicant membership, none of which have any Scriptural authority.

Fourthly, baby baptism is ruinous to the souls of thousands. Strictly speaking, it is not baby baptism but mistaken views regarding its efficacy and significance which leads multitudes down the broad way to destruction. William Cunningham observes:

> 'The tendency of these confused, erroneous, and exaggerated notions of the sacraments, is to lead men into the belief, more or less distinctly developed, that they are justification and regeneration, or, that they furnish evidence of the presence of these indispensable blessings, or, that they may serve as a sort of substitute for them. And, in one or other of these ways, we cannot doubt that the sacraments operate powerfully, in point of fact, in wrapping men in utter delusion about their spiritual condition, and in sending them down to destruction with a lie in their right hand. (*British and Foreign Evangelical Review,* 1860, p. 938.)

That plain people should be confused and deluded is not surprising when we examine some of the statements made about the efficacy of baby baptism. Take for example the Reformers. Consider the familiar words of the Prayer Book Service for the Public Baptism of Infants:

> 'Seeing now, dearly beloved brethren, that this child is regenerate' and later, 'We yield thee hearty thanks, most merciful Father, that it hath pleased thee to regenerate this baby with thy Holy Spirit, to receive him for thine own child by adoption, and to incorporate him into thy holy church.'

Then in the Catechism, the question 'Who gave you this name?' is answered:

'My Godfather and Godmother in my baptism; wherein I was made a member of Christ, the child of God, and an inheritor of the kingdom of heaven.'

Now can it be denied that these words are misleading? Is not the natural and unforced meaning of these statements such as implies baptismal regeneration? Bishop Ryle's explanation might untie this knot to the satisfaction of some, but the plain meaning of these words to the ordinary Christian is that babies are regenerated when baptized. Indeed, if a man believed baptismal regeneration, he would be hard put to it to find better words to express his belief than those in the Prayer Book. Hence the Evangelical Anglican who continues to use these misleading words must weigh the solemn possibility of being accessory to the eternal ruin of precious souls. As for current Reformed teaching which is not shackled to the Book of Common Prayer, even this is not wholly free from erroneous and misleading statements. Note the following from Pierre Marcel's *The Biblical Doctrine of Infant Baptism*:

'Baptism given to little children is the witness and attestation of their salvation, the seal and confirmation of the covenant of grace which God contracts with them.' (p. 213.)
    'Because of the promises of the covenant sealed by this baptism the parents and the church are strengthened in the faith which causes them to consider this baby as a child of God and a lamb in Christ's fold. They know that he no longer belongs to the race of Adam, that he is placed under the direct protection of the Lord, and that God loves him and regards him with affection. They know that this child is the heir presumptive of salvation.' (p. 225.)

Is it any wonder that Christians still think of baptism more highly than they ought to think?
    Concerning the state of affairs in the land of John Knox, Thomas Gutherie remarks:

'Prone as we of Scotland are, to boast that our fathers, with Knox as their head, came forth from Rome with less of her old superstitions about them than most other churches, to what else than some lingering remains of popery can we ascribe the extreme anxiety which some parents show to have baptism administered to a dying child? Does not this look like a rag of the old faith? It smells of the sepulchre ... Is there not reason to suspect that at the root of this anxious and unnecessary haste, there lies some lurking feeling that baptism — if not absolutely essential — is at least very serviceable to salvation, and has some connection, near or remote, with regeneration and remission of sins? Now with all respect and due regard to the feelings of those, from whose views on this subject we are constrained to differ, we cannot look upon such notions as else than the vestiges of an old superstition.' (*The Gospel in Ezekiel*, p. 238f.)

But what else can the people of Scotland be expected to believe when in the Shorter Catechism they are taught:

'Baptism is a sacrament, wherein the washing with water in the name of the Father, and of the Son, and of the Holy Ghost, doth signify and seal our engrafting into Christ, and partaking of the covenant of grace, and our engagement to be the Lord's.' (A. 94.)

Why not qualify this by saying that this statement only applies when baptism is administered to believers? (See Appendix C for some choice remarks by Cunningham.)

It is well known that conscientious Evangelical Paedobaptists spend considerable time preaching against baptismal regeneration and insisting upon the necessity of a personal conversion for salvation, and we cannot but hope that their words counteract the impression given by the wording of their official standards and services. But do they? Do their words really undo all the harm done? And if not, what must be said or done to dispel the delusion of baptismal regeneration? William Cunningham answers as follows:

'We believe that the notion of sacramental justification and regeneration, more or less distinctly developed, has always been, and still is, one of the most successful delusions which Satan employs for ruining men's souls, and that there is nothing of greater practical importance than to root out this notion from men's minds, and to guard them against its ruinous influence. This can be done only by impressing on them, right views of the sacramental principle, or the general doctrine of the sacraments, and applying it fully both to baptism and the Lord's Supper; and especially by bringing out the great truths, and that sacraments are intended for believers, that they can be lawfully and beneficially received only when faith has been already produced, that they imply or suppose the previous existence of the great fundamental blessings of remission and regeneration; while, at the same time, they do not, simply as external acts or providential results, afford any proof or evidence of the possession of these blessings, or the existence of the faith with which it is invariably connected. These views go to the root of the matter, and if fully and faithfully applied, would prevent the fearful mischief, which cannot, we fear, be reached in any other way.' (*British and Foreign Evangelical Review,* 1860, p. 939.)

The only effective way to prevent such a fearful mischief is to confine the sacraments — and this includes baptism — to those who profess faith.

Lastly, baptizing babies disgraces the name of Christ. The churches of Christ should be composed of all those who profess faith in Christ, but baby baptism opens wide the door to countless thousands who come to be regarded as part of the 'church'; and the result is that these baptized unbelievers bring the gospel into great disrepute in the eyes of the world. Not that any church of professing believers will be entirely free from occasions of stumbling, alas. But it will be much purer than the corresponding Paedobaptist church, and will thereby bring more glory to the name of the Saviour.

Conclusion

If, after due consideration of the evidence and arguments heretofore advanced, the reader remains persuaded that infant baptism is from heaven and not from men, he cannot help being grieved at what I have written. A lover of truth always hates error. It is no small sin to pervert one of the ordinances of Christ, and if I am guilty of such a sin, I trust he will pray God to grant me repentance unto the acknowledging of the truth. Perhaps he will attempt to show me wherein I have erred, and maybe someone will write an answer lest multitudes become ensnared through the circulation of this book.

But it may happen that the reader has been shaken by what he has read, and is now in great doubt concerning the origin of infant baptism. If so, let him read the book through again, remembering that every quotation comes from a Paedobaptist. If still unsettled, let him read all the books he can find on the subject, both for and against. Above all, let him prayerfully search the Scriptures again and again. It is his duty to study the question until he is fully satisfied in his own mind. So long as he has any doubts, he can hardly believe in or practise the baptism of babies with a good conscience.

Yet what I desire and what I have prayed for, is that the reader will have been convinced that baptizing babies is an unscriptural and anti-scriptural innovation, and an abomination of untold enormity. If this is the case with the reader, certain practical steps must result.

First, he will see that the baptism he may have received as a child is not a Christian baptism, and therefore he must needs be baptized as a professed believer if he is to keep the ordinance of Christ. This is a positive duty the neglect of which makes our love to Christ highly questionable, because 'He that loveth me keepeth my commandments.' If we call Christ, Lord, why do we not do the things he says?

Secondly, he will realise that he cannot continue as a Christian worker or minister in any church or denomination which makes baby baptism obligatory. It is a great pity that the Church of England for all its boasted comprehensiveness cannot embrace those unable to do such a small thing as baptize babies. How strange that a Church which can comprehend a Red Dean and an Infidel Bishop should be so intolerant of an Antipaedobaptist! But there it is, and the same intolerance is found in the Presbyterian denominations, so that an Antipaedobaptist can do nothing other than leave his denominational fold. To break from the church of one's fathers is by no means easy — I speak from experience — but whatever the temptation to compromise for the sake of supposed greater usefulness, we must remember that obedience is better than sacrifice.

Thirdly, the reader will now do all he can to show others the error of their ways. Not that he is to harp on this one string all the time. But if he is convinced that believers' baptism is a divine institution, he will be grieved and moved to action against the Reformed perversion of Christian baptism as much as our Reformers were against the Romanists' perversion of the Lord's Supper.

One last word to everybody no matter their convictions. Repentance towards God, faith towards Christ, love towards all the brethren, compassion towards the perishing — these are the things that matter most. Baby baptism is not unimportant — if I thought that I would not have spent so much time and labour on writing this book — but the kingdom of heaven is not baptism, whether baby or adult, but righteousness and joy and peace in the Holy Ghost.

Appendix A
Blessing of babies

The birth, marriage and death of people are events which are generally observed by holding a special church service, for which, however, there is no express Scripture warrant. Such services are deemed to be 'ordered by the light of nature and Christian prudence, according to the general rules of the Word.' (*Westminster Confession* 1. 6). They are not, however, of divine authority, and therefore are entirely optional. Scripture does not demand that a wedding be solemnized in church, or that it is necessary to have a funeral service. Nor does it require a Christian to bring his babies to any special service. But, as with marriages and funerals, so with births, it seems fitting that there should be some church ceremony to mark so notable an event.

The light of nature and Christian prudence has led some to adopt the practice of blessing babies which, be it said, should not be confused with dedication of babies. For the sake of those unfamiliar with the custom of a service of blessing, here follows an article by the author which was printed in the Summer issue of the 1960 Free Grace Record.

'In the gospels of Matthew (19:13-15), Mark (10:13-16), and Luke (18:15-17) we read of an occasion when Jesus took the little children up in his arms, put his hands on them, and blessed them.

1. Who brought their children to Jesus? We are not told. They might have been genuine believers in Christ or temporary followers.

2. How old were the children who were brought to Jesus? Matthew calls them 'little children'; Mark 'young children'; Luke 'infants' (or new-born babies).

3. Why were the children brought to Jesus? Matthew says 'that he might put his hands on them and pray.'

4. What did the disciples do? They rebuked those who were bringing the children, and tried to stop them coming to Jesus.

5. Why did they stop the children coming to Jesus? Because they thought that Jesus was not interested in babies who were not old enough to understand his teaching.

6. What happened when Jesus saw this? Mark tells us that 'he was much displeased'.

7. What did Jesus say to the disciples? 'Suffer the little children to come unto me, and forbid them not; for of such is the kingdom of heaven' or, in another translation, 'Let the little children come to me, and do not hinder them; for the kingdom of heaven belongs to such.'

8. What else did Jesus say? 'Verily I say unto you, Whosoever shall not receive the kingdom of God as a little child he shall not enter therein.'

9. What did Jesus do to the children? 'He took them up in his arms, put his hands upon them and blessed them.' We are not told that Jesus baptized the babies or christened them or dedicated them, but that he blessed them. Had Jesus baptized the babies the disciples would have protested even more, for they were accustomed to seeing the repentant baptized, but not babies.

10. What does 'blessed them' mean? Matthew says that the little children were brought to Jesus that he might put his hands on them and pray. To bless here does not mean to consecrate or dedicate, but to pray, asking God's blessing. Jesus blessed the children by praying over them and for them.

11. What did he pray for the children? We are not told, but whatever he asked of the Father he received, so that these children were blessed as a result of being brought to Jesus. Perhaps they were converted later in life. We are not told that Jesus'blessing the children made them Christians there and then.

12. What are we to do? We should bring our children to Jesus seeking his blessing upon them. He is the only Saviour, and he alone can save them from their sins.

We can bring our children to Jesus privately in prayer, which we should do constantly, but it is fitting that we should do this publicly as well — for the Lord is especially present in the midst of his people. If this is done, it is suggested that the minister read out to the congregation the above questions and answers in order to ensure the people understand the origin and nature of this blessing. Having done this, the minister takes the baby in his arms, and prays after this manner:

'Lord Jesus Christ, thou hast said that the kingdom of heaven belongs to little children, and we now bring to thee this child ... asking thee for thy blessing. Hear our prayers on his behalf, and in thy good time send thy Holy Spirit into his heart that he may be converted and saved from his sin, and be made a member of thy church and an heir of thy everlasting kingdom. Do this for thy name's sake. Amen.'

The service could well end with the blessing:

The Lord bless thee, and keep thee; the Lord make his face shine upon thee, and be gracious unto thee; the Lord lift up his countenance upon thee, and give thee peace. Amen.'

Appendix B
The Antiquity of the Baptism of Babies

A very fair review of the historical evidence respecting the antiquity of baby baptism is given by the Dutch theologian and historian, Venema:

'It is indeed certain, that Paedobaptism was practised in the second century; yet so, that it was not the custom of the church, nor the general practice; much less was it generally esteemed necessary that babies should be baptized... Tertullian has nowhere mentioned Paedobaptism among the traditions of the church, nor even among the customs of the church that were publicly received and usually observed; nay, he plainly intimates, that in his time it was yet a doubtful affair. For in his book, De Baptismo (chap. 18), he dissuades from baptizing babies, and proves by certain reasons that the delay of it to a more mature age is to be   preferred; which he certainly would not have done, if it had been a tradition and a public custom of the church, seeing he was very tenacious of traditions; nor, had it been a tradition, would he have failed to mention it ... It is manifest, therefore, that nothing was then determined concerning the time of baptism; nay, he judged it safer that unmarried persons should defer their baptism ... Nothing can be affirmed with certainty, concerning the custom of the church before Tertullian; seeing there is not anywhere in more ancient writers, that I know of, undoubted mention of baby baptism.

Justin Martyr, in his second apology, when describing baptism, mentions only that of adults. Irenaeus alone may be considered as referring to Paedobaptism, when he says, 'Christ passed through the ages of man, that he might save all by himself; all I say, who by him are regenerated to God, infants, and little ones, and children, and youths, and persons advanced in age.' For the word regenerated is wont to be used concerning baptism; and in that sense I freely admit may here be understood. Yet I do not consider it as undoubtedly so, seeing it is not always used in that sense, especially if no mention of baptism precede or follow; which is the case here: and here, to be regenerated by Christ, may be explained by sanctified, that is saved by Christ. The sense, therefore may be: That Christ's passing through all the ages of man, intended to signify, by his own example, that he came to save men of every age, also to sanctify or save infants.

'I conclude, therefore, that Paedobaptism cannot be certainly proved to have been practised before the times of Tertullian; and that there were persons in his age who desired their babies might be baptized, especially when they were afraid of their dying without baptism; which opinion Tertullian opposed, and by so doing, he intimates that Paedobaptism began to prevail ... These are the things that may be affirmed with apparent certainty, concerning the antiquity of infant baptism, after the times of the apostles; for more are maintained without solid foundation.' (Quoted in Abraham Booth's *Paedobaptism Examined* vol. 1 p. 370f.)

Appendix C
The Westminster Confession and Catechism

Besides having to modify the language of Scripture Paedobaptists are faced with the task of accommodating their own definitions of a sacrament. William Cunningham writes:

'The general definitions of sacraments and the corresponding general definition given of the objects and effects of baptism, do not apply fully and without some modification to the form in which we usually see baptism administered.' (*Historical Theology,* vol. 2, p. 145.)

Elsewhere Cunningham writes:

'It is impossible to deny, that the general description which the Shorter Catechism gives of a sacrament teaches, by plain implication, that the sacraments are intended only for believers, while no Protestants, except some of the Lutherans, have ever held that babies are capable of exercising faith ... Its general import, as implying a virtual restriction of these ordinances to believers, is too clear to be misunderstood or to admit of being explained away.' (*The Reformers and the Theology of the Reformation* p. 249f.)

'The Confession, c. 27, s. 1, lays it down as the first and principal end or object of the sacraments, of both equally alike, "to represent Christ and his benefits, and to confirm our interest in him," this last clause implying, that those for whom the sacraments were intended, have already and previously

acquired a personal interest in Christ, which could only be by
their union to him through faith. It further (sec. 3), in speaking
still of the sacraments, and, of course, of baptism as well as
the Lord's Supper, asserts that "the word of institution
contains a promise of benefit to worthy receivers;" and
worthy receivers, in the full import of the expression, are, in
the case of baptism, adult believers. In the next chapter, the
28th, the description given of baptism manifestly applies
only to believing adults. It is there described as "a sacrament
of the New Testament, ordained by Jesus Christ, not only for
the solemn admission of the party baptized into the visible
church, but also to be unto him a sign and seal of the covenant
of grace, of his engraftin into Christ, of regeneration, of
remission of sins, and of his giving up unto God through Jesus
Christ to walk in newness of life." It is quite true that babies,
as well as adults, though incapable of faith, must be engrafted
into Christ, and must receive regeneration and remission; and
that without this, indeed, they cannot be saved. But the
statement in the Confession plainly assumes, that each i n -
dividual baptized not only should have the necessary   pre-
liminary qualifications, but should be himself exercised and
satisfied upon this point, and should thus be prepared to take
part, intelligently and consciously, in the personal assumption of the practical obligations.' (Op. cit. p. 262f.)

In short, infant baptism is inconsistent with the definitions of
baptism as they stand. On the very next page Cunningham remarks
that 'error is generally inconsistent.' It certainly is!

Next we look at the proposed modifications in the case of infant
baptism.

'Men commonly, instead of considering distinctly what are
the necessary modifications of it, and what are the grounds
on which these modifications rest, leave the whole subject in
a very obscure and confused condition in their minds.'
(*Historical Theology*, vol. 2, p. 145.)

Most people are indeed confused, but is it any wonder when five
pages later Cunningham, in discussing the modification necessary
in the case of babies, declares:

'We are unable to put any such clear and explicit alternative in the case of the baptism of infants, or give any very definite account of the way and manner in which it bears upon or affects them individually. Men have often striven hard in their speculations to lay down something precise and definite, in the way of a general principle or standard, as to the bearing and effect of baptism in relation to the great blessings of justification and regeneration in the cases of infants individually. But the Scripture really affords no adequate materials for doing this.' (Op. cit. p. 150.)

Amazing confession! It is impossible to define the objects and effects of baptizing babies. No help is to be had from Scripture. Is it surprising that there is so much confusion on the subject? Even an expert theologian like Cunningham calls it 'a great difficulty'. Is this not further evidence that the baptism of babies is a departure from the simplicity that is in Christ?

One last quotation from Cunningham:

'It has always been a fundamental principle in the theology of Protestants, that the sacraments were instituted and intended for believers, and produce their appropriate beneficial effects, only through the faith which must have previously existed, and which is expressed and exercised in the act of partaking in them ... The disregard of it (i.e. this principle) involves them (i.e. the Confession and Catechism) in confusion, absurdity, and inconsistency.' (*The Reformers and the Theology of the Reformation*, p. 244f)

Baptizing babies is clearly a disregard of this principle, and hence all the confusion, absurdity and inconsistency.